THE BEST OF
REMINISCE

CONTENTS

REMINISCE

ASSOCIATE CREATIVE DIRECTOR:
Christina Spalatin
DEPUTY EDITOR: Linda Kast
ASSOCIATE EDITOR: Julie Kuczynski
LAYOUT DESIGNERS: Sabine Beaupre,
Payton Hintz
SENIOR COPY EDITOR: Dulcie Shoener
PRODUCTION ARTIST: Jill Banks
SENIOR RIGHTS ASSOCIATE: Jill Godsey

PICTURED ON FRONT COVER:
Playing London Bridge on page 25,
Joan Brandy
Leather, Strannik_fox/Shutterstock

PICTURED ON BACK COVER:
Car passengers on page 140,
Mark Steffen
Prom couple on page 61,
Cecilia Ann Francis
Serviceman on page 122, Weldon Reese

ADDITIONAL PHOTO CREDIT:
Vintage scrapbook page,
OHishiapply/Shutterstock

© 2019 RDA Enthusiast Brands, LLC.
1610 N. 2nd St., Suite 102
Milwaukee, WI 53212-3906

International Standard Book Number:
978-1-61765-846-4
International Standard Serial Number:
Applied for
Component Number: 117300062H

SINGLE FILE
These children of the 1960s cross the street in front of their school in an orderly fashion with the assistance of a very official-looking crossing guard. If only the dairy truck were an ice cream truck.
LARRY STEVENS · HATFIELD, PA

Take a walk down memory lane with us. We've selected the best of the best stories, photos and memories from the previous year of *Reminisce* magazine and compiled them here for you to enjoy and share with generations to come. There's something of interest for everyone!

The Best of Reminisce highlights the innocence of youth, fond memories of families with terrific photos from keepsake albums, and the excitement of true love. You'll also find some good ol'-fashioned fun, accounts of hard work by everyday people, stories of courageous animals during war years, Route 66 nostalgia, chance encounters with stars such as Mel Torme, and special holiday traditions with loved ones. Finally, laugh out loud at the antics in the last chapter, and get a kick out of large, colorful vintage ads sprinkled throughout the book.

Discover heartwarming happiness and so much more with *The Best of Reminisce*.

THE EDITORS OF *REMINISCE* MAGAZINE

CHAPTER 1

....

GROWING UP

Ah, to be a kid again! Experience the joys
and follies of youth with thoughtful memories
and fun photos from the past.

Hoops Pride

The Republic High School boys basketball team brought home its first
Class M State Championship in March 1963 with a win
at the University of Missouri–Columbia.

CINDY BROWN · SPRINGFIELD, MO

No Bush League Instructor

Mom was simply a natural at playing second base.

Mothers are complicated creatures. I found that out at 12 in 1950 when I had my first opportunity to play organized baseball. Our church, Caldwell Memorial Presbyterian, had decided to field a youth baseball team. We played other teams in the Charlotte, North Carolina, area.

Our uniforms were gray trimmed in blue with Caldwell on the front and our numbers on the back. I was number 10. I wore my blue cap everywhere and bought cleats with the money I earned delivering newspapers. I was excited to learn, but little did I know what I'd learn from my mother that summer.

The coaching staff found out rather quickly that I played infield better than I played outfield. They tried me at second base, but after the second practice I went home with dirt up my backside and my spirits lower than the spikes of my cleats. On every play, I was knocked flat.

As I got off my bicycle, my mom came out onto the porch. She took one good look at my dirty clothes and the expression on my face and asked, "What happened?"

After I told her, she put down her dish towel, came out to the yard, took my glove and showed

Harry's mom, Dessie, loved three things: her family, her church and her flower garden.

me how to play second base. She showed me how to crouch on the balls of my feet with the glove low and ready for a ground ball. She showed me footwork and how to handle an aggressive base runner.

The idea had never crossed my mind that my mom had played ball. So I watched, listened and practiced the footwork. There was more to this than I thought.

Then she sat down on the porch steps and told me a secret. She'd grown up in Indian Trail, North Carolina, and played second base for the high school girls softball team.

One day the boys baseball team played a game with the girls team. One boy tried to turn a single into a double and roared down the baseline toward the girl between him and the bag. My mother, the girl, decked him. From then on, everyone called her Deck. She never told anyone the story about her nickname because it wasn't ladylike to do such things.

I kept her secret safely locked in my heart until she passed away. When I revealed the story at her funeral, it brought smiles to many faces having a hard time trying to smile that day.

HARRY L. RAST JR. · NORTH CHESTERFIELD, VA

WHAT A CATCH!

OUR DAUGHTER CATHERINE, 8,
joined the spring fishing derby at Kirk's
Pond in Oxford, Connecticut, in 1972.
It was raining that day and she had a
pole with no reel—only a line and a hook.

Most of the other anglers fished
from the opposite side of the pond,
but Catherine wanted to be close to
me because I was in charge of hot
chocolate and doughnuts.

After fishing patiently for quite
some time, Catherine screamed with
excitement and pulled a big fish out of
the water. In fact, she caught the largest
fish of the day, and for her efforts she
won a fishing pole and spinning reel.

To top it all off, a picture of her with
her big catch made the front page of
the local newspaper.

PATRICIA CROWTHER
EDGEWATER, FL

Catherine holds her prizewinning fish for the camera.

THE SWING IN THE CELLAR

OUR SMALL ROW HOUSE HAD
barely enough room for living, let
alone for three children to play.
We went outdoors when weather
permitted, but if snow, rain and cold
kept us indoors, we were stumped.
Thankfully, my mother had a plan.
Our cellar, she mused, would make
the perfect playroom. The heat from
the coal furnace would provide a warm
refuge from the cold city street, and
with a few inexpensive improvements,
Mother was sure it could work.

She took an old woolen rug and
covered the floor in the new playroom.
She added two floor lamps and hung a
curtain in front of some storage shelves.
She placed our bookcase and toy box
along the wall. But the main attraction
was yet to come.

She sent us to the hardware store to
buy four thick metal bolts and a large
coil of heavy rope. My father attached
the bolts to the ceiling rafters, then
used the rope and some thick boards
to make two indoor swings.

The playroom quickly became a
neighborhood sensation. When Mother
offered homemade oatmeal cookies
and milk, the playroom was hard to
leave, no matter the weather outside.

DOROTHY STANAITIS
GLOUCESTER CITY, NJ

Dorothy holds
hands with
younger friends
in front of the
decorative grills
that opened to
deliver coal to
her basement.

A Bar Too High

When the coach takes a tumble.

Growing up in Floral, Arkansas, in the late '50s and through the '60s, I spent most of my time playing outdoors.

In those days, kids rode bicycles and climbed on trees, rocks or playground equipment. Spending time inside occurred mostly in winter when it was too cold to stay outside very long.

One summer around 1961 my parents bought me a metal swing set. I remember the day we received the big box of multicolored metal bars. My Uncle Emmett put the bars together to form the most beautiful, modern swing set I had ever seen.

I was so excited! I loved it and spent time on it every day. The set was such a grand improvement from the old rope swing I was used to, and I played on the slide, teeter totter or swing all the time.

When my cousin Teresa came over, the two of us played on it together. I was tall for my age and could jump up and reach the top bar and turn flips. Teresa was shorter than me and unable to master that feat. But because I believed I was such a brilliant gymnast, I decided to teach her how to catch the high bar and do flips, too.

In hindsight, she probably couldn't have reached the bar anyway, but I was determined that I could teach her.

"Do exactly like I do!" I said, convinced that I really was a star. I ran, took a giant leap, missed the bar completely, and landed flat on my back. Then, being in shock, I took a deep breath, but no air would enter my lungs. I lay there, gasping to breathe.

For the first time in my life I understood what the phrase "knocked the wind out of me" meant. I guess you could say my attempt to catch the high bar had left me totally breathless and grounded. The whole time, Teresa just stood there staring at me in amazement and fear. At that point, she was determined not to do *exactly* as I did!

ANGELINE BROWN STONER
FLORAL, AR

My attempt to catch the high bar left me breathless and grounded.

Angeline's new swing set delivered hours of outdoor fun.

Fistful of Pennies

A short bike ride turns into sweet satisfaction.

W henever my mind wanders and someone offers "a penny for your thoughts," I grin and think about a special place in Hilbert, Wisconsin. For those of us lucky enough to have grown up there in the 1960s and '70s, we had only to bike up Main Street to find the best spot in town—Krautkramer General Store.

It's 1968 and I'm a carefree, freckle-faced 8-year-old. St. Mary's is closed for the summer, and Mom has just brushed my hair into high pigtails and swabbed my sister Toby's knee with Mercurochrome.

She hands me a $5 bill and tells us to go to Krautkramer's for groceries. I ask if we can keep the change. (You see, Krautkramer's has the ultimate penny candy counter.) Mom nods and dries her hands on her apron.

With the money tucked in my pocket, Toby and I pedal off to the store. I pick up a loaf of Wonder Bread, summer sausage, stinky cheese and a six-pack of Fresca. Mrs. Krautkramer punches numbers into the big black cash register while her husband wraps the sausage before sliding it into our brown paper bag.

"Twelve cents back, dearie," says Mrs. K as she drops a dozen shiny pennies into my sweaty palm.

"Mom said we can get penny candy if there's change left," I tell her.

I got an A in second-grade math, so to be fair, Toby gets six pennies and I get six pennies.

"Wow, we're rich," Toby beams. Ten minutes later, Mrs. K drops our sweet treasures into two tiny brown bags and we plop our pennies onto the scratched wooden counter.

Skipping out the door, I see Mr. K hand a blue bottle of Windex and a roll of paper towels to his wife so she can get the candy counter ready for the next freckle-faced boy or girl who arrives with a fistful of pennies.

DARLENE BUECHEL · CHILTON, WI

Too Good Not to Share

A teenage boy, a disabled old woman and the special dog they both loved.

———

When I was growing up on the south side of Chicago in the 1950s, I had a pet collie named Lady. For nine years, Lady and I were inseparable and, at 14, I loved her with all my heart.

She had uncanny intelligence and instinct. She'd saved my little brother Ricky's life when he'd toddled into an alley just as a large truck was turning into the lane. Lady quickly ran to Ricky and pinned him up against a fence until the truck passed.

One day I went to do my paper route, leaving Lady in our yard as usual. Unfortunately, I forgot to lock the gate and she got out.

When I realized she was gone, I was devastated. For weeks, I searched high and low for her, to no avail. I had to resign myself to never seeing her again. My sorrow almost overwhelmed me.

Yet a few months later, while riding in my cousin's car several blocks from my house, I saw a man walking a dog that looked a lot like Lady.

"Stop the car!" I shouted. "That's my dog!"

I spoke to the man, who told me that the dog was his mother's; she'd had her for several months. He looked doubtful when I told him she was mine, so I turned to her and said, "Lady, come." She immediately sat next to me in the heel position.

"It appears she is your dog," said the man, who had found her wandering around his neighborhood and had taken her in. I was eager to get her home, so I agreed to go with him to break the news to his mother.

When we got to the house, Lady ran directly to the man's mother, who was in a wheelchair.

Lady had been the woman's constant companion since they'd found her, the son said, and had done wonders for his mother's attitude and life outlook.

It was clear by the way she sat so faithfully at the woman's side that Lady had bonded with her.

When the woman learned I was there to reclaim my lost dog, she began to cry. Her son, who was also now crying, apologized but insisted that they give Lady back to me.

By this time tears were streaming down my cheeks, too. I was faced with a terrible dilemma. I loved my dog and wanted her back, but I realized there was no way that I could take her away from this elderly woman who badly needed Lady's companionship. It would be selfish.

I told the woman she could keep Lady.

She and her son were full of gratitude and promised me that I could visit Lady whenever I wanted. But I knew that would only bring me more heartache. I knew, too, it was best for everyone that I stay away. Lady was performing an essential service now; she and her new owner deserved a clean break, without the worry that in a moment of longing I would demand my dog back.

Choosing to allow Lady to stay there was without doubt the most difficult decision I'd had to make up to that point in my life—and it was one of the toughest decisions I've ever made.

My tears flow once more as I write. I never saw Lady again, but I take comfort knowing that this incident helped to form my character, and that my cherished pet made the remaining years of that sweet old woman's life better.

MICHAEL STECZO · MILLIKEN, CO

There was no way that I could take her away from this elderly woman who badly needed Lady's companionship.

Lady smiles as Michael's beloved pet. She later brightened the world of a new owner.

The Spy Chasers at Summer Camp

A lonely cottage, mysterious lights and five very active imaginations.

When I was 10, I spent eight weeks at Camp Wahconah, a summer camp for girls near Pittsfield, Massachusetts. I didn't like it very much. It was too regimented, too competitive and too focused on athletics. But I did like the four girls with whom I shared a bunk and an unexpected adventure.

Our sleeping area was at the rear of the camp. Behind us were woods and, beyond the trees, an isolated summer cottage.

At night I watched the house from my bunk and noticed lights repeatedly going on, then off, briefly illuminating each window. I also saw what looked like a flashlight being clicked on and off in suspicious patterns.

I should add, this was 1943 and we were at war. There were rumors about German spies living in New York City and U-boats off the coast of Cape Cod. My young head was full of fears of evildoers and espionage.

One night, I told my four bunkmates of my worries. They quickly agreed the situation needed our careful attention. Appointing ourselves junior FBI agents, we'd slip out during rest hours and, using tree trunks for cover, spy on the "house of spies." We were convinced the light patterns were coded messages. We tried to decipher them but the code was complex.

At 10, Edith had a grand smile and a yen for intrigue.

Each time we ventured into the woods, we moved closer to the house. "We need a better look at the spies so we'll be able to identify them on wanted lists," I said. We even hatched a plan for two of us to knock on the door and claim to be lost, but we were too scared to carry it out.

One day in late August, we got caught in a downpour while maintaining our vigil. We decided to build a covering to protect us from the weather. We found a flat area free of tree roots, dug a large trench, stuck some branches into the ground and covered them with a piece of discarded linoleum.

The next time we arrived at the lean-to to watch our Nazis— for that's how we thought of them—we sniffed something foul. We had accidentally dug into a cesspool. That put a smelly end to our surveillance.

Soon after, it was time to go home. We never told anyone about the Nancy Drew Spycatchers Society of Bunk 12. But to this day I look back on it with astonishment and fondness. We'd turned an otherwise ordinary summer into something intoxicating, exciting and totally ours.

I wonder if the innocent vacationers staying in that house ever knew that they'd given us such a memorable experience?

EDITH SAMUELS
CINCINNATI, OH

We were convinced the light patterns were coded messages.

WHAT KIDS WANT

Colorful illustrations of smiling children help to promote products for kids.

1958 »

Sips in Summer

This Libby's ad is aimed squarely at busy moms whose kids spend their summer days working up a thirst running from one naughty prank to another. The "frozen" beneath the bright red Libby's logo is almost an afterthought—and why not? Who has time to wait for fresh-squeezed juice when there's a baby sister to tease?

« 1955

Coonskin Craze

Kids went wild for coonskin caps after *Davy Crockett* debuted on ABC-TV in 1954. Soon the caps were showing up in dozens of product ads, such as this one from 1955 for Karo syrup.

At night in downtown Sycamore, Illinois, in 1956, young people went to Teen Town for the music.

Schooltime vs. Summertime

During one's youth, the year is divided into two seasons.

G rowing up in Sycamore, Illinois, in the early 1950s was like growing up in Mayberry. The town's charm was as much a function of the times as it was the place. Although the Korean War was underway, those sights and sounds didn't invade our homes every night the way Vietnam did.

As teenagers, we had scant experience with class distinctions, racial injustice, unemployment or poverty. Maybe we were naive living in the American heartland, sheltered from the harsh realities of the world. Regardless, it was really a wonderful time to be a teenager, and Sycamore was the best place to live.

As in most small towns, schools were the center of community activity. We respected our teachers and they cared about us. In those days, a call from the school to a parent about a child's behavior or bad grades was taken seriously.

To be expelled was the worst. Yet, I recall one threatened expulsion that, in hindsight, seems unfair. John, a fine student and a solid citizen, was sent home for wearing sideburns. Remember, this was before Elvis or the Beatles were popular. John soon shaved his sideburns and returned to school.

Teen Town, Sycamore's recreation and social center, was established in 1953. Membership cost only a nominal fee, and the center was open several nights a week. We went there to dance, play Ping-Pong or hang out.

Few of us had jobs after school, but many young women I knew worked as carhops at the drive-in restaurants. The drive-in was another excuse to socialize, a place where boys and girls met, where friendships and romances bloomed.

During the summer, I detasseled corn for The Ag, the DeKalb Agricultural Association. The job lasted only a few weeks, but it was a quick way to make money for clothes and supplies for the upcoming school year. It also laid the foundation for my strong work ethic.

Summer was when I learned to play golf. If you lived in the Sycamore Park District, you could play rounds for free on Tuesday and Thursday mornings. After a few friends and I found some old golf clubs, we played there often.

If you or a parent worked for the Anaconda Wire and Cable Co., the park's outdoor pool was free, too. My sisters and I often hopped on our bicycles and rode there to swim for the entire afternoon.

The city's welcome sign once read "Life Offers More in Sycamore." It did in the '50s; maybe it's still true today.

GENE BEHLER
INDIANAPOLIS, IN

May 1954

SENIOR TRIP
MAC. ISLE

JOHN LESJACK

JIM EVERETT

CHUCK PETERS

JOHN FOW

1

2

3

MOM MADE IT HAPPEN

My father died when I was young, so when my mom came up with $48 for my senior class cruise on Lake Huron in 1954, I remember thinking how lucky I was. No matter the circumstances, my mother always came through for me. The SS *South American* was prepped for its first cruise of the tourist season, leaving from Detroit, Michigan, for Mackinac Island in Lake Huron and Canada's Sault Ste. Marie Locks that lead into Lake Superior. The three-day cruise was a perk for graduating from high school in Michigan in the early 1950s and was limited to 500 seniors.

JOHN LESJACK · SANTA ROSA, CA

1. On their senior class cruise in May 1954, clockwise from upper left, John Lesjack, Jim Everett, Chuck Peters and John Fow sit on the top deck of the ship. Tom O'Conner was the photographer. **2.** Seniors from East Detroit High School gather around the deck chairs. **3.** Friends since ninth grade, the self-styled Rugged Women of East Detroit High pose in front of a surrey while exploring Mackinac Island.

Strength of Spirit

Weighed down by braces on her legs, she stood taller than them all.

———

The first day of second grade in 1952 was the scariest of my entire life. We had just moved to South Carolina for my dad's job and we were living in a Spartan Mansion trailer instead of a house. I knew no one, not even my teacher.

When I walked into the classroom, a bit late, everything was in order. Mrs. Gattis had stacked each desk with books, our names on top. We were instructed to copy and take home the notes that covered the blackboard.

As May Day king of second grade, Lester escorts his queen, Diane, at their school in Jackson, South Carolina. A friendship rekindled once Lester and Diane connected and they could rehash their past (top right).

I took my seat, second row, third back, and I noticed an empty desk at the end of my row. Everyone was silently writing as I started my own copying from the board.

That's when it began. I heard and felt an odd *thump, thump,* rhythmic, like a metronome from music class.

The sound gradually got louder; the vibrations stronger. Distracted, I stopped and looked at the door. It was closed. Everyone else, including my teacher, took no notice. Then the noise stopped and the heavy oak door flung open so hard it hit the wall.

In came a tiny blond girl in a pink dress teetering on one stiff leg at a time. She walked by swinging her upper body back and forth. Strangely, whenever her foot hit the floor, a loud thump would emanate as if a sledgehammer had struck.

Later I learned she had a belt around her waist attached to iron bars that ran down the sides of each leg, connected by an iron bar under each foot. A polio survivor, she had no strength in her legs.

She started moving slowly down the row to my left. She hit each desk as she went by but the kids didn't react, just rearranged their disheveled books and kept writing. They all knew her.

As she got close, a boy in the next row slid his foot under hers without looking up or giving any clue as to his intent. It worked. The girl tripped and fell forward like a tree felled in the woods; her knees didn't bend. She desperately grabbed at the empty desk as she hit the floor, her books scattering.

I went from frightened to furious. I leaped to my feet and drew back; I wanted to hit the boy. I glanced at Mrs. Gattis, expecting a reaction. She sat oblivious, nose in her paperwork.

Surprised, I bent to help the girl. She shot me a furious look, her face

*Diane sped down the long hallway
on roller skates, hair and dress flying.
She zipped by in a rainfall of giggles.*

contorted. "I'll do it myself!" she hissed. I stood as she pulled herself up, leaned her back against the wall, compressed her dress around a knee and clicked the trip release on her braces. Then, grabbing her desk, in a quick motion she swung her heinie and sat down hard. I picked up her books and clumsily arranged them on her desk. With a deep frown, she muttered, "Thanks."

In time, Diane and I became friends. I admired the way she fought through her days with little or preferably no help. When her face was not contorted, she was beautiful. I often forgot about the braces. But I could not forget how my teacher never stepped in to help. I was mad, angry at her; I just couldn't understand.

Some time later my mom told me that we were invited to Diane's house. We pulled up to the new ranch-style home. The front door opened and Diane's mom gestured us in. The biggest surprise came when I realized that in the doorway hugging my mom was Mrs. Gattis. My teacher was Diane's mom.

We walked into the kitchen and I noticed that the new cabinets were dented all along the bottom. Then I heard the sound of ball bearings spinning. Diane sped down the long hallway on roller skates, hair and dress flying. She zipped by in a rainfall of giggles.

When she got to the kitchen cabinets, Diane caught herself with her hands, but she had no control over her feet. The heavy metal braces added momentum as her shoes splintered across the wood cabinets, fitting perfectly into the cabinetry indentations.

Mrs. Gattis paid no attention. She smiled, drank coffee and continued conversing with my mom. I then suddenly understood Mrs. Gattis and the classroom situation.

Diane's determination and courage at such a young age have always been an inspiration to me. I've told her story to people many times over the years.

My parents moved a lot when I was young, and Diane and I lost touch. Recently I found her using the internet and we reconnected after all these years.

LESTER BROOKSHIRE
ROME, GA

KIDDING AROUND

My mother took this photo of my sister (left), younger brother and me in 1951. As you can see, it was windy that day on the farm in Kimball, South Dakota.

SUSAN ANN PIBAL · PIERRE, SD

LIKE GRANDPA
My father, Gabby Gebhardt, passes on his love of DIY to my son Jonathan in his New Jersey home's amazing workshop around 1986.
PHYLLIS GEBHARDT · KISSIMMEE, FL

THE COCK-A-DOODLE-DOO
My husband, Edward, raised chickens as a boy. Here he is during World War II with his favorite rooster, Tojo.
GWEN ASPLUNDH
HUNTINGDON VALLEY, PA

THE BATHING COMPANION

When I was a girl, I didn't play with dolls; I had my bantam chickens. This photo is from the mid-1940s when I was about 4. Whenever Mom gave me a bath, my little hen Bitsy would watch from her perch on the closed lid of the toilet.

JUDY PEARCE · CARPINTERIA, CA

KIDDING AROUND

Brenda and I have been friends since third grade, when her family moved to Westchester, New Hampshire. Here I am with Brenda (right) and her sister DeDe.

MARILYN MONS
MANCHESTER, NH

THAT'S MONKEY BUSINESS

My father-in-law, Donald Neilson, who lived in Los Angeles in 1939, told us about an organ grinder who would visit his neighborhood. When the kids heard him coming down the street, they would beg their parents for money, then hurry outside with their change. The man had a little monkey who ran around and collected money. Here, the monkey embraces Donald before returning to the organ grinder with the money.

JAMIE NEILSON
TRABUCO CANYON, CA

REACH FOR THE SKY

With shows like *The Lone Ranger* popular in the 1950s, it's no wonder my friends and I liked to play cowboys. I'm in the back with a pair of six-shooters.

RICK HNATH · NORTHVALE, NJ

ON STAGE

I was in fifth grade in McLean, Illinois, in 1947, when several one-room schools put on a joint musical. Based on the costumes, I think it was *Old King Cole*.

MARY NELSON · WEST LAFAYETTE, IN

KIDDING AROUND

GRIDIRON GOLIATHS
We were all-American kids, in sixth grade at Stanley Hall School in Evansville, Indiana, in 1963. From left, Jimmy Kappenman, Frank Johnson, Christopher Clayton and Eric Johnson; with the pigskin, Ernie Rogers and David Wilder.
REV. DAVID M. POLAND
LANSDALE, PA

Shirley, 10, Valerie, 4, and Glenn, 5, pose after raiding the attic one day in 1967.

DORIS JOYCE · LACONIA, NH

My cousin Arvid Miller and I were fishing in 1940 on Oak Lake, Minnesota, using tree branches for makeshift poles.

DOROTHY McCUNE
PARADISE, MT

MY FAIR LADY
I had endless fun playing London Bridge with my older sister
Helen and our friend David in 1950. My grandma Rose Applebaum
snapped the photo in Bliss Park in Brooklyn's Bay Ridge area.
JOAN BRANDY · BROOKLYN, NY

The Brauer boys, Chris, 10, and Ben, 8, captured in a rare filial embrace in the 1980s.

Wheel of Fortune

How a car tire set them on the course of their lives.

My younger brother Ben and I grew up across the street from a large park in a quiet neighborhood of Victoria, British Columbia. Our house was below street level, which meant that all groceries, camping gear, decorative rocks and anything else our parents made us haul had to be heaved up and down the steep front lawn, because the car was always parked on the road.

Like many children of the '80s, we spent Saturday mornings watching cartoons and enjoying sugary cereal. At some point before lunch, our mother would turn off the TV and shoo us outside.

One particular morning, she sent us to help our father change a car tire. Watching him get his hands dirty and swear under his breath was somehow considered male bonding. Eventually, he bestowed on us the responsibility of inching the old tire, rim and all, down the driveway and into the garage while he went inside.

It occurred to me that there might be a more efficient way to get the job done. An episode of *He-Man and the Masters of the Universe* was starting soon and I didn't want to miss it. My plan was to roll the heavy tire down the driveway and Ben would catch it. I didn't take physics or biology into consideration. I was just thinking about myself. And He-Man.

I sent Ben down to stand in the garage. I had him shuffle to the left and then a bit to the right until he was exactly at dead center. Then, closing one of my eyes to aim, I pushed the tire steadily into motion. I was quite proud of myself. As the thing picked up speed, I nodded in a self-congratulatory way.

Only when it neared the halfway mark did I suddenly realize that I might have been wrong. As the tire rolled faster and faster down its path of doom, with Ben standing there, arms outstretched like some sacrificial offering, I imagined the rest of my life as an only child.

Then something I can't explain happened. As the tire got closer to the garage it wobbled ever so slightly, changing direction. Rather than barreling into Ben, it hit the door next to the garage. In fact, it blew the door off its hinges.

Though I was relieved that my brother wasn't crushed, I knew the noise would bring our parents storming out, and Ben, who was 8, wasn't yet smart enough to lie. I was grounded. No *He-Man* or any other TV for a month.

I think of this incident with the tire as a defining moment for both of us. Ben is now an engineer and I bury myself in words as a writer. My brother chose to focus his life in the world of physics, and I chose to focus mine in the arts, where I can studiously avoid physics.

We haven't looked back since.

CHRIS BRAUER · CRESTON, BC

Chugga Chugga!

My dad, David Hutchinson, 2, plays choo-choo train on a footstool with
his older brother, Eddie, in their backyard in Altadena, California, in 1942.

SUSAN HUTCHINSON · SAN DIMAS, CA

CHAPTER 2

ALL IN THE FAMILY

Being part of a family comes with some
responsibility, but mostly big smiles
and lots of love all around.

MAY · 55

Sunny Smiles

I snapped this picture of my family enjoying the bright weather and warm
sand at the point in Orient, New York, on Long Island's north fork.

BILL LARSON · BATAVIA, IL

Family Expansion

With a little remodeling and many helping hands,
this quartet beat the odds.

O n May 3, 1950, shortly after I turned 8, my mother, Dolores Seifert, gave birth to quadruplets. She was 37 and apparently perimenopausal.

Back then, there were no fertility drugs, and hospitals and doctors didn't have access to ultrasound equipment. Instead, they took an X-ray and saw three babies. But when it came time to deliver, Mom and my dad, Arthur, were surprised by a fourth child.

She was supposed to deliver in New Ulm, Minnesota, which had a better hospital than the one in our small town. But she ended up at the Sleepy Eye hospital before she went into labor and stayed there because they couldn't move her to New Ulm. Hospitals during that time had no neonatal or intensive care units,

so it was a miracle that all four babies were born alive and flourished.

Overnight we went from a family of eight— Mom, Dad, four boys and two girls—to 12. Our new siblings consisted of three girls and a boy: Monica Mae, Martha Ann, Marie Dolores and Michael Arthur. Each weighed between 2½ and 4 pounds.

Companies from as far away as Massachusetts donated items to help my parents take care of the quads. There were four cribs in the nursery, a custom-made baby buggy and four high chairs. Feeding all of them in their high chairs at the same time was a chore.

Before the babies came home, Dad turned our screened porch into a sleeping room with the baby cribs on one side and a bedroom on the other.

At the Minnesota State Fair, above, people paid 25 cents to see the quads when they were babies. Dolores and Arthur Seifert, top right, made room for specialty furnishings and four of just about everything, including clothes, cribs and high chairs—plus one custom-built carriage.

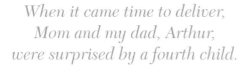

When it came time to deliver, Mom and my dad, Arthur, were surprised by a fourth child.

My older cousins helped by cleaning the house or cooking for us. Women from the Twin Cities (Minneapolis and St. Paul) came and helped on the farm. My folks also hired a nurse from Florida to help care for the foursome. She influenced me to go to nursing school; later, my sister Monica went to the same school.

People from across the country came to our farm for a peek at our baby sisters and brother. We received mail from other countries, too.

Their birthday was a special day, and often the quads got the day off from school and went to the movies together or to a Twins baseball game courtesy of Ernie Fliegel, owner of the 620 Club, a Minneapolis restaurant.

VIOLA SEIFERT LEFF · WALKER, MN

The Seifert quads grew up like most other kids of that era. They had chores to do but found plenty of ways to have fun.

Grandma Baba kept the farm running smoothly while Grandpa Zedo worked in the coal mines. At right, big sister Loretta steadies her baby sister Dorothy as they play outside in the grass at Baba and Zedo's house.

This Happy Home

Yearly visits to grandparents' farm transported them to a simpler time.

Each year my family took an annual trip from our home in Canton, Ohio, to visit our paternal grandparents, who lived about an eight-hour drive away in the coal-mining town of Hawk Run, Pennsylvania. Grandma and Grandpa lived on a small farm in a two-story house that was situated in a fork of the road.

Zedo (Grandpa) was a coal miner and a joker. Baba (Grandma) was a homemaker and a farm lady. Besides being the chief cook, she also fed the chickens, weeded the garden, milked the cow, and made the butter and cheese. If we were fortunate enough to be there when she milked the cow, she would pour a glass of warm milk for my little sister and me and say, "Drink."

The old farmhouse was more than a little primitive, with no gas or running water. It did have electricity, however, and a water pump in the kitchen for cooking and for weekly baths taken in a wooden tub in the storage room.

We used an outhouse for nature calls. In fact, that's where we kids learned to read the Sears catalog. At night we put a pot under our beds for emergencies.

The house had no furnace, only a wood-burning stove with four burners and an oven. My grandparents used the stove to heat the house and for cooking and heating bathwater.

We rarely made the trip to Hawk Run in winter, but I remember one night tucked in bed under a down quilt that Baba had made. When I woke in the morning, there was ice on the window.

The happiest place in the house wasn't even inside the house. It was on the front porch. My sister and I would spend hours there, swinging on the porch swing and singing songs. Sometimes after he got home from the mines, Zedo would sneak up behind the swing and yell "boo!" We cried and ran to Mom.

Memories—such happy ones—were made there. The house now is for sale and has all the modern conveniences, but we have all the memories.

LORETTA BECHERUCCI
BAKERSFIELD, CA

Family Fun Time

Pride and place kept everyone together.

A ll seven of my aunts and uncles lived close to us in Dallas, Texas, where I grew up in the 1950s and '60s.

I could ride my bike to four of their houses. We had wonderful family gatherings on Thanksgiving, Christmas and Easter, and birthday parties almost monthly.

In spring, after we'd finished our meal the guys would go outside to play football. My uncle was a high school football star and I thought no one could throw a pass like him.

Sometimes we even let our aunts play.

Another uncle would stand on his head in the middle of the living room floor. I'm not sure why he did this, but I was impressed. A third uncle managed the first grocery store in town that sold nonfood items. One cousin was a cadet at Texas A&M and wore an official-looking uniform, while another was a school librarian. And another cousin had a '57 Chevy that sped down the street like a rocket—that is, if his parents weren't around.

In the summer, we'd make ice cream. My sister and I would take turns cranking the machine, sitting on it for ballast. The cousins also got in on the act. We played the whole time we were together, while the grown-ups talked and did boring adult stuff.

When I got a little older, I began to really appreciate those gatherings. My aunts made amazing desserts and served sweet tea. My uncles would take afternoon naps, which sounded boring back then, but perfect now.

Oh, how I miss those days.

STEVE MELTON
DALLAS, TX

DRESS CODE

DO YOU REMEMBER when Sunday afternoons were for hunkering down in someone's yard and for catching up on the week's news?

While the men played horseshoes, the women brought out the croquet set. Kids jumped rope, shot marbles, played tag and badminton, or dug in the sandbox.

Food was the main event, of course, and the attire was nothing like it is today. There were no jeans, just casual pants and button-down shirts for the men, and cotton sundresses were *de rigueur* for the ladies.

I was a real camera buff in 1958 and looked for opportunities where I could. When my dad and his brothers-in-law sat in our backyard in Trooper, Pennsylvania, chewing the fat over a beer, I took my chance.

RUTHMARIE BROOKS SILVER
EAGLEVILLE, PA

From left, my father, Gerald Ward Brooks, and my uncles William Harold Deihm Sr., Irvin S. Lownes Sr. and John Rutherford Phillips didn't even flinch when I snapped this photo with my Kodak box camera.

11/24/15

Dear Grandma,

You have made a big change in my life, which I thank you for it. Now, I will tell you that every time you do something nice for me, I've been taking note of it in my heart. Here are just a few of the many numorous times that I've seen it.

First of all, when I used to come home from school, and mom was working, you would always have a snack and a warm, smiling face for me. After that, you would help me with my homework. When that was finished, we would always play board games like Scrabble or Battleship.

Then, another time was when Hurricane Sandy hit our house, and we lost electricity, there was your house to go to. Lastly, whenever we had a piano recital, performance, or graduation, you would always be there to lead us on.

To wrap it up, I am trying to thank you, and I love you, our grandma who has been there to show us you care.

Love,

Sinclair

A LOST ART

I was surprised when I received this letter from my young grandson Sinclair, telling me how much he appreciated me and itemizing the things I had done for him.

ANN GUIDA · LIVINGSTON MANOR, NY

With that big smile and his kind nature, Sinclair melted his grandma's heart.

It's the Little Things

Living in the moment, enjoying simple pleasures and cherishing time spent with loved ones will create lasting memories.

When I think back on those who influenced me and made me the person I am today, I think of my Gramma B (to distinguish her from my other grandmother, Gramma R). My father's mom, Gramma B had four boys. I was her first female grandchild and a real delight to her.

As a grandmother myself now, I can appreciate the connection a grandmother has to her granddaughter. She gladly baby-sat for my parents. When I was under 2, she kept me at her house while my mother had back surgery.

My grandmother was born in the 1800s and lived to be 99; she passed away in the 1970s. She taught school at a one-room schoolhouse and, after marrying my grandfather, lived and worked on the family farm. She would regale us with stories of the olden days when they rode into town to buy groceries during winter in a horse-drawn sleigh covered with heavy robes. How I wish that I would have had her write those stories down for me.

My grandfather died when I was a toddler, and after that Gramma B lived alone in a small house nearby. Her house was filled with antiques and a cookie jar that was always full. She tended a garden and shoveled her own snow until she was well into her 80s.

During vacations I would stay at her house for a day or two. Sleeping in her four-poster bed was a treat. When I was old enough, she let me wind her mantel clock with a big key. She convinced me that dusting was a game, and I would dust the furniture just for fun. According to Gramma B, doing housework and making cookies to fill the cookie jar came before play.

Thinking of her Gramma B reminds Shirley of the strong connection between generations.

Fun often involved card games. Her favorite one was Flinch. The game involved card piles similar to solitaire; the object was to use up all your cards. We played for hours, sometimes forgetting to start dinner. She never let me win, demanding a rematch if I did.

Thinking of her always brings a smile. She was tall—5 feet, 9 inches—and her hair was gray and neatly combed. Her face looked stern, but she smiled with delight when we visited. She taught me to age gracefully and carry myself with dignity and calm.

On my dressing table is a silver mirror she gave me inscribed with her initials. Whenever I look at it, I feel as if she is there looking over me. Sometimes I think the world would be a better place if we shut off our cellphones and played Flinch for the afternoon.

SHIRLEY MYERS · VALATIE, NY

Edwin lived to laugh, while Pauline looked for the best in them all.

GOOD, CLEAN ADVICE

HAVING BEEN BORN IN 1933, I LEARNED ABOUT
values from my parents during a much simpler time. My
mother, Pauline, kept our small home spotlessly clean. She
believed that cleanliness was next to godliness. Her advice
was "Always wear clean underwear in case of an accident"
and "Keep yourself clean and neat." She was caring and
loving, but a little lacking in the humor department.

My father, Edwin, on the other hand, had enough wit
for them both. He was humble and people-oriented and
loved to sing and tell funny stories.

His advice: "If you meet someone without a smile, give
him/her one of yours" and "Always treat everyone the way
you want to be treated.
Be honest and truthful
and don't forget to laugh
at yourself sometimes."

Their advice served
me well, and I'm thankful
I could pass on these
nuggets of wisdom to my
three sons, who grew up
in a very different world.

IRENE SULLIVAN-HERNANDEZ
DELMAR, MD

Taking a cue from her dad,
Irene offered a smile to everyone
she came in contact with.

ONLY THE BEST

My father passed away when I was
12 and my brother Bob was 8. After
that, my mother packed us up and we
moved from Chicago, Illinois, to nearby
Blue Island to live with her mother,
Grandma Link. Mom went to work at
the local City Hall and Grandma took
care of us. She got us ready to go to
school on time, did chores around the
house, made sure our homework was
done before suppertime and played
games with us. She even taught us
to be good sports. She was the best
grandma you could have.

WOOTSIE REIHER
BLUE ISLAND, IL

MOM'S NEW ICEBOX

A big hand for the prettiest appliance in the house.

Pick a Color from the Rainbow !

Color-Keyed to Your Kitchen !

INTERNATIONAL HARVESTER Refrigerators

Exclusive with International Harvester! Gorgeous color comes to refrigerators, to make your kitchen sing with a gleaming color accent! Ten brilliant colors to choose from —in cleverly designed, changeable door handle plaques to fit any color scheme.

they're femineered ..!

. . . and YEARS AHEAD! Chore-savers by the score! Spacious shelves of chrome or stainless steel! Pantry-Dor, Bottle Opener, Butter Keeper, full-width Freezers, Coldstream Crispers, Egg-O-Mat! Seven sizes, seven prices. See them, NOW!

International Harvester Also Builds Home Freezers . . . McCormick Farm Equipment and Farmall Tractors . . . Motor Trucks . . . Industrial Power

1951 »

A Splash of Color

Appliance makers saw the new army of homemakers in the postwar years as a gold mine. International Harvester said that its products were "femineered" with women's needs in mind, such as space efficiency for those tiny housing-boom kitchens. In 1951, the company had a stroke of genius: color! A simple swap of a door handle turned a fridge from drab to fab.

SEE THE NEW GIBSON

WITH EXCLUSIVE NEW

Swing-out Servers

PLUS

Automatic Defrosting

FREE! Accept this exciting

3-bottle Harriet Hubbard Ayer

Cologne ACCORDION

Gibson SINCE 1877

REFRIGERATORS · ELECTRIC RANGES · FREEZERS · AIR CONDITIONERS

« 1953

Swingin' Style

Along with timesaving automatic defrost, this Gibson model boasts other female-pleasing innovations: an interior in "cameo cream" and see-through bins that swing out for easy access to the food. The perfume set for visiting a dealer is similar to toy promos popular among carmakers of the time.

A Journey Out of Salt Lake

While following her dream, she stayed true to her homespun roots.

My cousin Jean Willes always wanted to be a movie star. Born in Los Angeles in 1923, she grew up in Salt Lake City, where her father worked and where the family practiced its Mormon faith. Like me, she came from Mormon ancestors who crossed the plains in wagon trains and settled in the Salt Lake City area. Her mother, Velma, and my Grandfather Bert were siblings.

Jean moved with her family to Seattle when she got older. In 1943, she made her film debut in *So Proudly We Hail* and moved back to Los Angeles. Meanwhile, my family settled in Denver. My mom always kept in touch with our cousin Jean. Eventually, Jean married an NFL football player, Gerard Cowhig, and together they had a son, Jerry.

Over three decades, Jean became a fairly big star. I was always fascinated with her movie career. Every time a show she appeared in came on our black-and-white TV, I'd be glued to the set.

I convinced my mom and dad to take a trip to Hollywood to visit her in 1962, when I was 14. Jean and her husband had a lovely home and pool, which my brother and I enjoyed.

Jean was very down-to-earth, kind and beautiful. She never lost her humble beginnings, even though she was part of the socialite circle.

Before we left, she gave me a big hug and said, "Honey, always follow your dreams."

She passed away in 1989, but I've always remembered her advice and the kindness she showed to a young girl.

JULIE NATALE MANN
CENTENNIAL, CO

CLOSE-UP: JEAN WILLES

Born: April 15, 1923, in Los Angeles, California
Died: Jan. 3, 1989

....

Appeared in more than 200 movies, film shorts and TV shows.

....

Starred with Lorne Greene, Clark Gable, James Garner, Andy Griffith, Frank Sinatra, Angie Dickinson, Ernest Borgnine and the Three Stooges, among others.

....

Movie appearances:
The King and Four Queens, Gypsy, Invasion of the Body Snatchers, Ocean's 11, No Time for Sergeants

....

TV appearances:
Zorro, Bat Masterson, The Twilight Zone, Peter Gunn, Perry Mason, The Jack Benny Program, 77 Sunset Strip, Bonanza, McHale's Navy, Maverick, The Beverly Hillbillies

A casual visit in Jean's backyard includes her son, Jerry; her mom, Velma; Jean; and author Julie.

Iris discovered that the Strawn sisters, June, Jodie and Fran, were her first cousins once removed.

Oddly Familiar

Relatives can live in the same town and not even know each other.

S everal years ago, my Uncle Ken informed me that a man in Tennessee had compiled a volume on the Hartsell family. My great-grandmother's maiden name was Hartsell.

So I wrote the man, Larry Fox, and he sent me a copy of the Hartsell volume. He also asked additional questions about my immediate family that he wanted to include in a subsequent genealogy report.

As I looked through the names in Larry's volume, I focused on those descended from my immediate ancestors. I found one name I instantly recognized: Fran Dumas. Fran was the secretary at my church, and I knew her well. As it turned out, she and I were first cousins once removed. Her mother was my grandmother's first cousin.

I reached out to Fran and excitedly told her of my discovery, and we marveled that we were cousins. We would never have known any of this if I hadn't read Larry's publication.

Later, my husband, James, daughter Amy and I visited Larry and his wife, Maggie, when we passed through Tennessee on vacation. Maggie was the Hartsell descendant, and Larry the genealogy sleuth.

I also got to know Maude, Fran's mother, who lived in Kyle, a little town a few miles south of us in Texas. She remembered my grandmother and great-grandmother and thrilled me with family stories, one about a table that was brought in a wagon from Oklahoma to Austin. Two leaves of the table cracked when the wagon got stuck in the mud. Maude is now deceased and I have moved away, but Fran and I stay in touch through Christmas cards.

IRIS SUMMERS
FORT WORTH, TX

RMS *Titanic* left port in Southampton, England, on April 10, 1912, never to return.

Tales Worth Sharing

Personal stories bring family history to life.

R aising two daughters has given me plenty of excuse to tell stories— some funny, some sad and some of interest only to the family. My mother told me a few; my father, the rest.

I've always been fascinated by one story about my father as a teenager. He traveled by himself from Hungary when it was still part of the Austro-Hungarian Empire. He was supposed to sail from Hamburg, Germany, to England and, once there, get a third-class ticket to sail in steerage on the *Titanic*. We've since learned that people in steerage, below the *Titanic*'s decks, had the lowest survival rate. Yet by a quirk of fate in my dad's travel plans that kept him from sailing, we are here to tell his story!

Another story is how my grandfather, the mayor of a rural Hungarian village, saved a Jewish storekeeper from a bunch of angry, intoxicated soldiers. Armed only with a chair, courage and a gift for words, Gramps diffused a very bad situation. Later, that storekeeper's son helped my father get his traveling papers to America.

Then during the Great Depression, just before my parents lost their farm in Pennsylvania, a traveling salesman came to the door. My mother felt sorry for him, so she bought some cheap brushes she had no use for and gave him the few dollars she was saving for a dress. That memory makes me very proud of her.

My folks came from a place and time that had no TVs or radios, so storytelling was important to them. My siblings (there were 10 of us) grew up listening to all kinds of stories. The ones we liked best always had a supernatural twist.

Whether you handwrite, type or download your stories onto computers, record the family history as best as you can. Some day in the future, new generations are sure to enjoy them.

TOM R. KOVACH
NEVIS, MN

Which Winslow Was It?

Research clarifies family members' historical claims.

———

All families have stories about their ancestors passed down through the generations. But discerning how true the stories are requires a bit of research.

My paternal grandmother, Clara Shannon Seavey, claimed that her mother, Isola Winslow Shannon, was a direct descendant of a Mayflower family, the Winslows. Thanks to a genealogical search on *Ancestry.com*, I was able to verify this—but only partly.

My research showed that, indeed, there is a line that goes back to the Winslows, but not to Edward, the Winslow on that first ship. (Edward was elected governor of the Plymouth Colony settlement three times and is mentioned in many history books.) My family traces its roots to a younger brother, Kenelm Winslow, who came on a later voyage to join the colony. In addition, I've found lines going back to the Mayflower through different great-grandparents: one to Gov. William Bradford, longtime governor of the Plymouth Colony, and another to John Alden and Priscilla Mullins Alden.

Interestingly, one of my aunts, my mother's brother's wife, also claims descent from the Aldens. So that means my cousins are both first and distant at the same time. It's funny how deep those New England roots can run.

GARY E. SEAVEY
SACO, ME

Above left, Isola and Joseph, Gary's great-grandparents, ride in the back seat while their daughters Ina and Clara sit up front and Clara's beau, Edgar Seavey, leans on the door. Grandmother Clara (above right) loved to share stories.

GROUP SHOT!

SHORT AND SWEET
Two of my three daughters were still growing into their perfect smiles in 1978. Valarie, 17, is finally out of braces; her sister Dorinda, 15, endures her braces; and 6-year-old Valinda is missing two front teeth.
JOYCE CASE
NEW IBERIA, LA

STRIKE THE POSE
Snapped at Chestnut Ridge Park near Buffalo, New York, during the summer of 1948, we Machowski girls—from left, Lorraine, 10, me, 5, and Barbara, 8—had the moves. Later in life, friends and family called us the Gabor sisters after Zsa Zsa, Eva and Magda.
SANDI KINTZEL · CLARENCE, NY

My sister, Dotty, and I embrace in this 1948 photo. At the time, I'm sure, my momma made me do it, but now we are really close and talk weekly on the phone.

JIM VANCE
TUSTIN, CA

FAMILY BAND

This picture from 1958 reminds me of how our careers started. I was a singer for 35 years (shown here on banjo). My dad, Pott Folse (accordion), still performs, brother Rick (sax) plays nine instruments, Ronnie (trumpet) plays keyboard and Steve (trombone) is a drummer.
DEBRA CHIASSON
RACELAND, LA

SAND AND SUN

On a summer vacation to Maine's York Beach in 1944, my sister Molly (left) and I loved to build moats as the tide came in. Molly was 6 and I was 8 at the time.
CARLA RITTER
IVINS, UT

GROUP SHOT!

Dad taught me to never give up on my goals and to respect and love my family. Here I am in 1949 at 8 months in Dad's arms at my grandmother's house in Linesville, Pennsylvania.

KATHLEEN McDONALD
ERIE, PA

POSING PROGRESS

My wife, Veri, and I got caught in a playful moment (above) as we tried to set up a picture with our new baby and our dog. A few years later, we posed with our children, Mindy Sue and David McKinley, for a formal photo. The dachshund stayed home for that one.

DAVID BUTTON · ROSWELL, NM

This picture of my wife, Jeannine, and me with our sons Mark, Ron, Steve, Jeff, Tim and Bruce ran in the 1965 directory for First Church of the Nazarene in Kokomo, Indiana.

ROBERT HOSTETLER · KOKOMO, IN

IN LIVING COLOR
We liked bright fabrics in my family. This photo of my parents, Steve and Cheri; my brothers, Zach and Nate; and me (on Mom's lap) is from 1992.
CHASE PATT
NORTH FOND DU LAC, WI

Lars hugs Lady, who hugs Chris.

Lady Was a Lucky Find

A beloved pet strengthens our hearts, opens our minds and brings out the best in us.

M y dog's story begins at the Gold Trail Hotel in Ilford, Manitoba, a tiny village pasted to the side of the railroad that ends at Churchill, on Hudson Bay. As the Polar Bear Express thundered past, I reminisced with Kip Thompson, the hotel's owner, about the pup he'd sold me in the late 1960s.

She was supposed to be a shepherd/Newfoundland cross like her older siblings. The mother was definitely a shepherd, but the Thompsons weren't sure about the father. I called my wife, Sally, who said, "Well, OK. Gee, maybe not. I wonder if we should?" I took that for a yes, so I lured the scrawny pup out from beneath the hotel, where she'd been surviving on fish guts after her mother had been shot. I paid Kip $50 and carted her off to my seaplane, the *Tundra Cub*.

One problem remained: what to tell the customs agent at the U.S. border. I didn't know the regulations for importing dogs, and I didn't want to detour to Kenora, Ontario, to get her shots, but I knew it would be stupid to try to hide her. I decided to let the agent conclude that my pup was returning to the U.S. At customs, I plunked her down in front of the inspector and began to secure the Cub. He gave the plane a cursory check, then turned to the dog. "Got any papers?" he asked.

"No, I don't," I said with a look of puzzlement. "But they didn't ask for any on the way out."

"Well," he said, "she looks OK, so you can go."

That night, I took Lady into the shower and washed off about 10 pounds of dirt from an 8-pound dog.

She matured into a beautiful German shepherd, the guardian and friend of my wife and our sons, Christopher and Lars, and my best buddy for 11 short years. When arthritis finally crippled her, I carried her to my veterinarian's office. There, as I cradled her in my arms, an injection stopped her heart.

On the long drive home, I fought tears and the ache in my throat. Unable to continue, I pulled to the side of the road, lowered our station wagon's tailgate and buried my face in her still-warm fur. My grief poured out.

Many years have passed, but were it possible, I'd gladly pay $10,000 or more to buy back that $50 dog.

GEORGE ERICKSON · EVELETH, MN

Fireside Chat

Our family loved to camp—around our home state of Wisconsin
and on trips to Virginia and Canada to visit relatives. In 1963, my wife,
Joyce, and our kids, from left, Steve, 11, Ann, 9, Mark, 5, and Robin, 3,
relax with Joyce's parents, Joe and Gertrude Foltz.

BRUCE THOMPSON · WAUKESHA, WI

CHAPTER 3

TRUE
LOVE

Take a look back on longtime loves,
chance encounters, stylish weddings
and amusing dates.

With Six You Get Marriage

When my cousins arranged a blind date for me with John Olliges, I was shocked. I knew his wife had died two days after giving birth to their sixth child. I told them I didn't want to go out with a man with "all those children." Well, he was a really nice guy, and we went on another date and another, until I finally said yes to his proposal—the night before Mother's Day.

CAROL OLLIGES · LOUISVILLE, KY

Everett's favorite photo of Sara shows her charm and style.

Sara's favorite photo of Everett shows his true nature and love of life on the farm.

Second Time Around

After a decades long delay, those early sparks reignited.

———

Back in 1946 when I was 17, my daddy bought some standing timber that he cut and trimmed, selling the remaining logs for wood. He hired a handsome young man, Everett, with a long-bed truck to haul the logs away to their destination.

Because my three sisters were much older and my two brothers younger than me, I was often elected to help Daddy with projects like this. He had me drag the trimmed branches to a pile for later disposal. It didn't take long, however, for Everett and me to notice each other.

The weather in our part of Illinois had been rainy and the gravel roads were hard to use. Everett's truck got mired in mud, but he quickly found a way to get out on his own. Dad admired his prowess; I admired his brawn.

About that time, the local high school was planning its prom festivities, and although I badly wanted to go, I didn't have any prospects. The prom king had been coaxing Everett to ask a girl so he could join the friend and his date. Everett was somewhat reticent because he wasn't seeing anyone special at the time.

A few nights later during dinner, a big truck drove into our yard. It was customary for the man of the house to go out and greet the person rather than have the driver come to the door, and Dad came back with a grin a mile wide on his face, announcing: "He doesn't want to talk to me. It's Sara he wants to see."

I hurried outside and returned giddy with excitement. I had an invitation to prom with Everett.

The next several weeks were spent finding a dress for the occasion. I had no idea what to expect but

The world stood still.
Somehow I floated across the aisle and sat down
next to him, grabbing his hand.

was pleased when Everett showed up with a beautiful bouquet of gardenias. Neither of us was very experienced with dancing, but we had no trouble finding things to talk about.

After the dance we went to a local ice cream parlor, and I felt I had found Mr. Right.

We dated until I graduated from high school and went to secretarial school in Rockford, Illinois, about 30 miles away. The school arranged for me to live with a family there. I earned room and board baby-sitting their son. I took the bus home on weekends, and Everett brought me back on Sunday nights. Inseparable, we spent all our time together.

Soon, however, I outgrew the school and decided to quit and go to work. I had tasted city life and favored it over the hard work on the farm. The family I stayed with often suggested that I date other boys.

I knew Everett was a farmer and no doubt would plan his future around farming. I began meeting new people through work, and as both of us started dating others, our dates grew fewer and further apart. Soon I found out that Everett married a high school acquaintance of mine.

I moved to California with a friend and started work at a loan company. There I met a young soldier who had recently completed six years in the Army and had lived in an area of Illinois close to my home. We were married, but it didn't take long to see my mistake.

Eventually I relocated to Denver, Colorado, where I worked in the state Supreme Court. Everett moved to Colorado as well and became a successful mechanic, starting his own business. He served as chief of the fire department in his area, and for many years as a deputy in the sheriff's department.

Neither of us knew we were living only 60 miles apart. Whenever I visited my family in Illinois and asked if anyone had seen or heard from Everett, I always got the same answer: No.

Then in 1991, both Everett and I visited Illinois at the same time. My mother, sister and I had an early lunch at the only restaurant in town. It's a small town and everyone knew my mother, who was delighted to introduce her daughters, calling

us by name. I nudged her and said, "I wish you wouldn't do that. If there's someone in here who knows me, I'd be so embarrassed."

Across the aisle came a voice: "Well, do you know me?"

"Should I?"

"Probably not," came the reply.

"Who are you?" I wanted to know.

The response: "Everett."

The world stood still. Somehow I floated across the aisle and sat down next to him, grabbing his hand.

It didn't take us long to go over the past 45 years and renew the same sweet feelings we'd left behind. We exchanged information so we could get together once we returned to our homes in Colorado.

Now Everett is 90 and I am 88. We hope to celebrate our 26th wedding anniversary soon.

SARA STRAW · MARYVILLE, MO

That chance meeting in November 1991 rekindled Everett and Sara's relationship, which had begun 45 years earlier.

Just married, Betty and Blanton pose for a kiss on June 16, 1957.

Stuck in Gear

His quick exit plan ran into a snag.

On Father's Day 1957 in the small southern town of Sturgis, Kentucky, a double wedding ceremony featuring two popular sisters got top billing. I was one of the lucky grooms, about to marry lovely Bell sister Betty.

The day turned out to be one of the hottest of the summer. There was no air conditioning and only limited parking at the First Christian Church, yet attendees came from far and wide. But it was the wedding's end that had everyone talking for weeks.

My initial plan was to get through our vows, finish some punch and cake at the reception, dash to a nearby neighbor's house to change clothes, pick up my new wife and speed away to Kentucky Lake Resort 90 miles south.

You see, the draft board had selected me to report for duty at Fort Knox in three days. My goal was to have the honeymoon of a lifetime and make the most of three nights with my honey. I could scarcely imagine the kind of devious plans my buddies and cousins had in store.

When we left the side door of the church on that Sunday afternoon, I could see that my Chevy Bel Air had signs painted across its side and a string of cans and bottles tied to the rear bumper. Relieved to be leaving the pressing crowd of well-wishers who'd pelted us with birdseed and rice, I opened the passenger door for Betty and then climbed in the driver's side.

Unfortunately, when I started the engine the car didn't move an inch. Peeking out the window, I could see cameras flashing and people cheering and laughing.

Then it hit me. Someone must have deflated my tires. I jumped out of the car and looked around, but none of the tires was flat. On closer inspection, though, I could see that both rear tires had been elevated off the pavement.

Oh, dear! I thought. *Has someone actually blocked up my wheels?* Sure enough, there were concrete blocks on either side of my rear axle.

Well, there went my well-planned strategy for a quick getaway. For the next 30 to 40 minutes, the crowd grew to watch me jack up the car and remove the blocks.

Fortunately, the honeymoon was a different story. All my expectations were met. We've now celebrated more than 60 years of wedded bliss.

BLANTON CROFT · HAGERSTOWN, MD

Let's Get Serious

Meeting at a funeral launched a whirlwind relationship.

———

While at work, I got a call that my grandmother had passed away suddenly. That evening, my family met at my aunt's house. The men were seated at the dining table, with me at the far end facing the door into the living room. I looked up to see three women standing in the doorway. One was my mother, but I had never seen the other two, a middle-aged lady and a teenage girl.

The woman turned out to be my dad's cousin, and thus my grandmother's niece. The teenage girl was this cousin's niece. Her aunt had brought her to pay her respects to my grandmother's family.

Without my knowledge, the girl started asking my mother questions about me. She asked if I was married, to which my mom replied, "Honey, he's not even serious."

A few days went by and I made it my business to find Louise, the lovely young lady from the funeral. I discovered she worked in the candy department at Sears. In those days, department stores did not have high shelves as they do today, so you could walk in the front door and see across the entire store.

The candy counter was rectangular, with candy bins all the way around, and the clerk worked in the middle. I entered the store and made my way to the girl of my dreams. I asked her for a date and she immediately accepted.

That began a whirlwind courtship, and five months later we were married. For the next six months I teased my bride and almost had her believing we were cousins.

The truth is, we were not related at all. Her lineage is traced on her aunt's mother's side and I was on her aunt's father's side. The aunt just happened to be the link between both families.

To complicate matters even further, Louise's mother died two years after my father died. A couple of years later, her dad and my mother were married.

Now I could kid her that we were more than just cousins; we were stepbrother and sister.

HAROLD TABB
NAVARRE, FL

Now I could kid her that we were stepbrother and sister.

Married in 1964, Harold and Louise are still just kids at heart.

Six States and a Thousand Miles Away

They made it work no matter their surroundings.

Born in 1930, my mom, Gwen Doutt, was a fun, outgoing person and well-liked by co-workers, friends and members of her church. My dad, Bernie Speth, was six years older and loved telling stories about his childhood. The couple were introduced in 1948 or '49 by mutual friends Dale and May Schreckengost.

Dale and my dad had served in the military during World War II. After they returned to the States, my dad went back to the grocery store business in Titusville, Pennsylvania. In 1948, Mom graduated from high school in nearby Franklin and went to work at a bank in that town. Twice a week, Dad would drive his produce truck to Cleveland, Ohio. Every once in a while, if their schedules allowed, Mom would ride with Dad in the truck. You might call this their premarital courting ritual.

After a short engagement, Mom and Dad married in April 1950, a few months shy of her 20th birthday. The wedding took place at Rocky Grove Avenue Presbyterian Church in Franklin, where my mom was an active member.

They drove to Florida for their honeymoon. Years later, they recalled how they both got sunburned so badly that for three days they looked like lobsters.

Soon after, Mom left the bank and joined Dad in running their own produce market in Franklin, called Speth's Market. My brother, Dave, was born two years later, in 1952.

But opportunity knocked, and the following year the family moved to Fort Worth, Texas, where my dad took a job with Chicago Pneumatic Tool Co. when it opened a new plant there. My sister, Nancy, was born in Texas in 1961.

Six years later, Mom and Dad prepared for another big move and returned to Franklin, where I was born in 1967. Dad worked as a computer programmer until 1986, when he retired. My mom worked at a tax bureau and the county courthouse until she retired in 1988.

My parents were married for a total of 62 years. They traveled many miles together and always had time for their family and friends. Mom died in 2012 and Dad in 2015.

JAMES SPETH
FRANKLIN, PA

Exchanging glances, Gwen and Bernie Speth depart on their honeymoon.

Over the Moon

Wild rides and tender moments gave teens a thrill.

This souvenir photo taken in 1955 shows Don and Pat riding the moon at Riverview.

Growing up in Chicago, Illinois, in the 1950s, I spent many days and nights at the now-defunct Riverview Park on the city's north side. My teenage memories of that era involve me, my wife and our friends.

To celebrate my birthday, for a couple of years my Grandmother Vivian took me and a group of my friends on an outing to the amusement park. We took a streetcar, known to us as the Red Rattler, north to the park. There we'd eat a picnic lunch in the grove and spend the day on rides and playing carnival games. After we'd gone through all our money, we'd head back home on the streetcar.

During those years, I had an after-school job, and when I earned $5, I thought I was rich. My favorite ride was the Bobs, a renowned wooden roller coaster famous for its speed and its 85-foot drop.

When I turned 16, I met Pat Hansen, a girl two years younger than me. A neighbor who went to Visitation High School, the all-girl Catholic school Pat attended, brought her over to meet me and my friends. We fell in love at first sight.

After that we spent many dates going to Riverview, and even had our picture taken there. We always ended the night watching fireworks and taking the Red Rattler home.

Pat and I married in 1959 and spent 55 happy years together until she died in 2014.

I still keep in touch with many of the people who went on those Riverview outings. We get together a few times a year and mostly talk about the days gone by. We grew up in the ideal era to be a teenager.

DON MILLER
LIBERTYVILLE, IL

Cross-Cultural Courtship Blitz

Once their paths crossed, being together was all that mattered.

When I joined an international pen pal club in November 1959, I had no idea how it would change my life. I was an RN at a large hospital in Bremen, in northern Germany. By December, the letters started pouring in. One letter from Sweden piqued my interest. It was from a Swedish horticulturist who lived and worked in Helsingborg. He wrote the letter in German, and soon many more of his letters crossed The Sound, or Oresund, and the Baltic Sea.

Around Easter in 1960, Nils wanted to meet. He arrived on Good Friday. On Saturday, we took a 20 km hike in rainy April weather to Worpswede, a famous artist village in Lower Saxony, Germany. In the evening we visited the world-renowned Ratskeller in Bremen, which housed Europe's oldest wine barrel, dated 1653.

By this time, it was not only the wine that had warmed our hearts. Nils proposed, and we planned our wedding in Sweden for Midsommar (midsummer), a joyful annual holiday in Scandinavia in late June. Two days later, Nils flew back home and I was left to plan the wedding by mastering piles of paperwork and fighting bureaucracy.

Now what? I did not speak Swedish and so I decided to cram in 10 hours of Berlitz language lessons a week before the wedding.

We drove to Helsingborg, where the marriage took place in a beautiful old *kyrka* (church) with Nils' family and a few friends present. My father was still in East Germany, behind the Iron Curtain. To this day I do not know what the pastor said, but according to the certificate we were married!

At the end of 1962 we moved to Encinitas, California, to establish a flower

Elfriede and Nils found a common language when writing letters back and forth.

business for a well-known Swedish grower. Nils built the business and eventually purchased it from his boss, changing from carnations to roses shipped around the U.S.

We became U.S. citizens and adopted two children. Nils and I did a lot of volunteer work in the community and received many awards.

Nils died at home in 2004 when he was 82. We had a blessed 43-year marriage after our Swedish/German courtship blitz.

ELFRIEDE LUNNERDAL
SAN MARCOS, CA

Reverse Migration

A new life began in her grandparents' homeland.

My seven siblings and I grew up on a farm in southern Wisconsin. Dad's parents, who emigrated from Norway, also lived with us. Our grandparents spoke longingly of what they called the old country, describing Norway's majestic mountains and fjords—and the siblings left behind.

In 1960, when I was 10, my oldest sister, Audrey, embarked on an unusual adventure for a woman in her early 20s. She and our cousin Nancy traveled by ship to Norway. There they bought bicycles and spent three months traversing southern farmlands and northern fishing villages, over the mountains and along fjords.

When summer ended, Audrey was in love with Norway and not ready to leave, so smitten that she arranged to work at a youth hostel in the Rauma Valley. In exchange, the owners' teenage son, Hans, would return home with her the following year to experience life on a Wisconsin farm while attending high school.

At the hostel, Audrey became acquainted with Arne, a good friend of her Norwegian hosts. Everyone in the village enjoyed listening to his stories, and this included Audrey, even though she didn't understand his Norwegian.

Despite the language barrier, they were drawn together by a shared passion for music, mountains and fjords. And as Audrey learned the language, their friendship grew.

Dressed in traditional Norwegian garb, Audrey and Arne wed in 1962.

One spring day Arne invited her to join him for a Sunday drive with friends from England. It never occurred to her that the invitation was anything more than showing an American tourist the countryside, or that visiting his family was for the purpose of introducing her.

The trip made her realize they had even more in common. Like her, Arne was one of eight siblings and grew up on a farm.

But after 10 months, the time had come for Audrey's fairy tale to end. She had to leave with Hans.

Driving to Oslo, where they would board the ship, Hans decided that his girlfriend, Arne's niece, should take the train to send them off. After their goodbyes at the dock, she could ride home with her uncle. Alas, the ship sailed before anyone arrived.

Day turned to night as their ship sailed down the Norwegian coast, making a last stop hours later in Kristiansand before heading to the U.S. As the ship docked, Audrey and Hans could not believe their eyes. There stood Arne and his niece on the pier, waving.

She knew he drove fast, but this was unbelievable! Arne rushed to Audrey before she got down the ramp. As they embraced, people watching from the sidelines clapped for their joyous reunion.

The farewell was magical as Audrey reboarded the ship, now wearing a thin gold band.

ARVID BERGE
MADISON, WI

Too Embarrassing to Resist

She wasn't wild about Harry at first, but he kept popping up.

M y sister Diane had a date with a fellow, Omelan Mycyk, for a high school graduation dance in Chester, Pennsylvania, in 1963, and Omelan brought his best friend, Harry, to be my date. Harry was a gentleman, for sure, but at 6 feet 1 inch, he was too tall for me. I'm barely 5 feet. He was very skinny, which made him look even taller. He was blond, and I liked brown hair.

We went dancing and he was good at it—so good that he was doing splits and stuff like that. It was a bit embarrassing. I was having a good time, but it felt awkward being with such a tall guy. We'd pass by windows and I could see how huge he was compared to me.

Harry asked me out for the next night, but I'd accepted a blind date with a boy named Tony. He was a lot shorter than Harry and had brown hair. To my surprise, Harry showed up at my door the next night anyway, and we all ended up going to a dance together. It was embarrassing, to say the least, but since we were all blind dates, we weren't invested in each other. At the end of the night, Tony kissed me good night—and so did Harry.

I asked Tony to my graduation party. We went on a few more dates, but that was it. Meanwhile, Harry would knock at my door now and then, and we'd go for a walk or have dinner. Harry didn't talk much. I wasn't into Harry.

He showed up one day when I was ice skating. He'd never skated before, but he bought new skates and walked several miles to the lake to skate with my sister and me. Two hours later, he walked home. My father gladly would have driven him home, but as I said, Harry didn't say much, and he certainly didn't ask for favors. I always knew, however, how he felt about me.

In the summer, my sister and I were at the shore with family when Harry and his father drove up, towing a boat. We invited them to stay the night, and the next day, they taught us to water-ski. What a blast, though it still was embarrassing because they'd invited themselves. By then, though, Harry was growing on me.

Years passed, and Harry joined the Army and went to Vietnam. We corresponded and got to know each other much better.

Conversation had never been Harry's strength, but he wrote meaningful letters. By the time he got out of the Army in 1970, it no longer mattered to me how tall he was or that he had blond hair.

We have been happily married now for more than 45 years. Harry is the best thing that ever happened to me.

NANCY FIRKO
CLAYMONT, DE

Harry, a tall drink of water, grew on pint-size Nancy.

A Roller Coaster Ride to Her Heart

He fell, big-time, for that little lady.

A n the Fourth of July in 1947, my mother, Dorothy, was not looking forward to spending the holiday with her two little brothers at home in Burbank, California. She was 17. She wanted to have fun. Her friend Faye called to say that her boyfriend had a friend, John, from Montana, who had recently completed a tour of duty in Japan. Now training to be an aviation mechanic, John needed a date for the day—would she come along? Mom was shy about going on blind dates, but because the alternative was worse, she said yes.

They went on a picnic at Griffith Park, then to the zoo, and wound up at the Santa Monica Pier, where there was a carnival. At the target-shooting booth, John easily won Dorothy a treasured stuffed animal. As they walked, he reached out and took her hand. Years later, Mom remembered how their hands seemed to fit together—it felt right to her.

They decided to ride the Blue Streak Racer. John had never been on a roller coaster before, but he eagerly boarded one of the cars with Dorothy sitting close by. As the coaster took off with a *click-click-click*, she glanced at John, anticipating the first drop. But John looked as if he was wondering what he'd gotten himself into.

The cars plunged down the first grade and zoomed around curve after curve as the riders screamed and cheered. Back at the depot, Dorothy exited the ride and turned to look at John. Just as he stepped off, he passed out!

My 5-foot-5-inch mother helped my 6-foot-3-inch father as he crumpled to the deck. She held his head in her lap, brushing his hair out of his face. As she watched his eyes open, all she could see was how blue they were, and she knew then that this was the man she was going to marry.

She took him for a walk on the nearby beach to clear his head as holiday fireworks went off in the background.

Faye confessed to my mother the next day that she had tried another friend before she called Dorothy but had gotten a busy signal twice. Faye had never expected Dorothy to agree to a blind date, but she'd called her anyway.

That date lasted: Dorothy and John were together for 54 years.

Dorothy and John married on Sept. 19, 1948, at the Little Church of the Flowers at Forest Lawn, California. My two brothers and I would not have been born and I wouldn't have been able to share this sweet love story if it weren't for a busy signal many years ago.

KATHLEEN M. VARELLA
NEW BRAUNFELS, TX

A CINDERELLA STORY

My friend Debbie and I both had single mothers. Living on tight budgets meant no extra money for prom dresses. But Debbie's granny was a seamstress and made us dresses using satin remnants. Dinner was at The Islands in San Diego, California, and dancing was at El Cortez, a beautiful landmark hotel. The night was perfect and I didn't want it to end.

JUDI CARROLL · ESCONDIDO, CA

Ralph, Debbie, Judi and Bill of Helix High's Class of '65 enjoyed prom night. Judi's date, Bill, looked like a model in his rented tux on that fairy-tale night in May, and Judi's wrist corsage matched her dress.

Romance was in the air, but not when they said goodnight.

TEAHOUSE OF THE SENIOR PROM

The boy next door, Wayne Thomas Marshall, asked me to his senior prom at Normandy High School near St. Louis, Missouri, in May 1965. The prom's theme was Teahouse of the August Moon after the movie of the same name.

I bought my dress from a secondhand store for $15 and my Aunt Agnes sewed 2-inch straps to the bodice.

Wayne picked me up in his 1957 red and white Chevy. Afterward we cruised Steak 'n Shake and went bowling—yes, in our prom clothes.

No goodnight kisses—although he liked me, he was, after all, just the boy next door.

CECILIA ANN FRANCIS · BALLWIN, MO

THE ROMANCE OF AVON

Print ads lay foundation for door-to-door cosmetic sales for easy beauty.

1957 »

Collectible Allure

Avon started in the late 1800s as the California Perfume Co., and fragrances have remained a product line mainstay throughout the company's history. When Avon learned that its scent bottles were becoming collectors' favorites, it began featuring those products more prominently in ads, as in this one from *Household* magazine.

« 1951

A Natural Beauty Queen

Barbara Ann Scott, known as Canada's Sweetheart, became a young idol at 19 when she won figure skating gold at the 1948 Olympics in St. Moritz, Switzerland—on an outdoor rink, no less, pockmarked from two hockey games. By 1951, she was starring in a popular touring ice revue. With her poise, fresh looks and name recognition, Scott covered two Avon ad campaign topics of the period, heroines and Hollywood stars.

BOOKLETS OF LOVE
Vintage valentines from the 1940s certainly say it with charm.
I found these storybook-style cards among my parents' belongings.
Note the signature at the end: *Love, Precious Fuzzy Wuzzy.*
CAROL BYRON · EAST WILLIAMSON, NY

IN LOVE

THRILLING RIDE

In my senior year of high school in 1948, a friend asked me to a tobogganing party her mother was throwing for some local boys who'd helped her. They were all nice boys, but a red-haired, good-looking one named Wendell—Bunk, as he was known—caught my eye. Two years later, we married. That blind date on a toboggan made our future.

JOYCE GRUMMET · JENISON, MI

TRENDSETTING HUES

My mother, Ethel Blome, married my father, Charles Roedersheimer, on Nov. 21, 1940, a time of year when yellow flowers were the only fresh ones available. Her attendants were her sister Deloris in blue and my dad's sister Martha in pink. I think they wore different colors because there were just the two bridesmaids in the wedding party. I have always thought their dresses to be unique.

LOIS DOBRADENKA
SHELBY TOWNSHIP, MI

I see us outside St. Mary's on that October day in 1982. Rich pops the champagne as everyone cheers our newly wedded life.

DARLENE BUECHEL · CHILTON, WI

SHARED ANNIVERSARIES

The first of October is a special date for descendants of Dewey and Ruth Bunner, who were married on that day in 1916. Since then, five couples in their extended family have married on Oct. 1, including the three pictured here. Harriet Bunner, Dewey and Ruth's daughter, married Herbert Dady in 1937 (lower right); Barbara Bunner, Harriet's sister, married John Shinn in 1949 (left); and Timothy Dady, Harriet's son, married Maureen Kay Moran in 1968. The most recent Oct. 1 weddings in our family were Tim Dady Jr.'s marriage to Hope Howard in 1998 and Annette Leschewski's to Douglas Taylor in 1999. Annette, my daughter, is the granddaughter of Harriet and Herbert.

JUDY DADY LESCHEWSKI · DECATUR, IL

Sidney scooped up Shelly in his arms and carried her home.

Friendly in Flatbush

His pickup line proved quite literal.

During my last year of junior high school, in 1958, we moved to a neighborhood in East Flatbush/Brownsville, Brooklyn, New York. It was rough at first, but I finally made friends with a girl named Sarah and often visited her after school.

After I made a few trips to her family's apartment, Sarah asked me if I'd like to meet her friend Sidney, who lived in the building next door. I agreed, not thinking too much about it. A few days later I was at her home when she looked out her kitchen window and said, "He's here."

"Who?" I asked.

"Sidney," she said. "Let's go!"

There he was, standing outside her window. *What a macho guy,* I thought. His dark, wavy hair curled down the center of his forehead, similar to the style Fonzie wore on the TV show *Happy Days,* only this was well before that time.

I swooned and tried not to show it as Sidney and I made casual conversation about his exploits the day before in the schoolyard where, according to him, "the guys tossed around a girl they knew like a football."

"What do you mean?" I asked, rather naively.

I don't remember whether I was just startled or totally impressed.

"Like this," he said, and he lifted me up. "We're going home," he added. I asked Sarah if it would be all right with her if we left. I suspected that she also had a crush on Sidney.

"It's OK," she told us.

My home was a few blocks away, and he carried me as if I was a featherweight. Once there, we sat and talked on the bench outside. My mom saw him from a distance when she returned home and told me later that she thought I was talking to a teacher. He looked much more mature than I did.

When he told me he was 17 and asked my age, something told me not to say 14½. So I said I was 15.

The next day he told Sarah he wanted to call me and "drag me to the beach." So, she gave him my number.

We looked at romance differently then, that's for sure. But this was the real thing. Sidney and I were married in 1965. After being married to my macho guy for more than 50 years—and three children later—I can truly say he's been the best husband that any gal could possibly have.

SHELLY SITZER · CHARLOTTESVILLE, VA

A Night to Remember

Three things I remember from prom on May 14, 1944: my date's name, Gordon May; where it took place, Hotel Argonne in Lima, Ohio; and what I wore, a pink satin formal with a borrowed fur jacket. After 74 years, how can anyone expect me to remember all the things that took place back then?

LEE WILLIAMS · LIMA, OH

CHAPTER 4

RETRO FUN

Relive the pleasures of days gone by when
a game of Scrabble or racing in a Soap
Box Derby brought out our best.

Daily Dipping

Summers in the city were spent at the community pool, where kids young
and old soaked up the warm sunshine and splashed in the cool water
for hours. My Uncle Merle took this photo on a hot day.

CHUCK BELLING · MADISON, WI

Performers at Weeki Wachee Springs in Spring Hill, Florida, hold air hoses that allow them to breathe and remain submerged for programs lasting up to 45 minutes. Visitors filled the 400-seat auditorium to watch the underwater ballet.

A Dream Ripples Through Time

One showman's innovation left a deep impression.

Central Florida in the 1950s and '60s had many roadside attractions, including Marineland, Silver Springs and Cypress Gardens, but my favorite was Weeki Wachee, a theme park built around a freshwater spring in Hernando County.

Seated in the auditorium, with its large picture windows that looked into the depths 16 feet below the surface, I was mesmerized by women dressed as mermaids performing underwater ballets. While submerged, the mermaids could eat a banana and drink from a soda bottle.

For weeks after our visits, I'd practice the mermaids' moves in our pool at home. I even learned to eat and drink underwater, too.

I didn't have to go far for help mastering the tricks. My father was Newton A. "Newt" Perry, who founded Weeki Wachee in 1947.

Newt was an innovator and performer. He got into show business in the 1920s doing short documentaries with Grantland Rice, a popular sportswriter whose Sportlight Film shorts would run in movie theaters before the feature.

Newt went on to be technical adviser on the *Tarzan* movies and a stunt double for actor Johnny Weissmuller in the 1930s. And in World War II, he trained frogmen, members of the Navy unit that grew into the SEAL program.

But my father's dream was to build an underwater attraction. When he opened Weeki Wachee, he did the shows there with a few local women he recruited to be mermaids. He taught them to breathe using air hoses hidden around the underwater sets, a technique that allowed them to remain submerged for up to 45 minutes and which is still used at the park.

It's remarkable that Newt's dream continues more than 70 years later. Now a state park, Weeki Wachee still has the power to mesmerize anyone lucky enough to visit there.

DELEE PERRY · OCALA, FL

THE PAST SPRINGS ETERNAL: WEEKI WACHEE THEN & NOW

The Seminole name Weeki Wachee means "little spring" or "winding river."

....

The spring is believed to be the deepest in the U.S. Its caverns have been explored to a depth of 407 feet, but the bottom hasn't been found.

....

The spring pumps about 117 million gallons a day of fresh, 74-degree water into the Weeki Wachee River, which wends 12 miles to the Gulf of Mexico.

....

Submerged signs warn divers away from its most treacherous caves. Certain areas can be explored only during droughts, when the current slows down.

....

When Newt Perry scouted the area for his roadside park in the '40s, the spring was clogged with appliances, old cars and other junk.

....

Perry built his auditorium into the spring's limestone shelf. It forms a natural theater on a slope 16 to 20 feet below the surface, where the current is a robust 5 mph. Mermaids work hard to stay in place.

....

The first show was Oct. 13, 1947. Mermaids weren't paid, but they did get free meals and bathing suits.

....

In 1959, steady promotion by new owner ABC kicked off the park's most successful period.

....

It joined Florida's state park system in 2008 and has a $13 adult gate fee. Mermaids perform three times daily.

Newt Perry before and after Weeki Wachee: setting up a unique picnic for a 1942 short film (top); and with daughter Delee and wife Dorothy in 1970.

Electric boat tours of the canals at Cypress Gardens provided intimate views of tropical flora. The tours started in 1937 and remained popular throughout the park's history.

Where Wishes Were Free

A day at Cypress Gardens offered a peaceful retreat from war.

L ocated in former swampland along the shore of Lake Eloise in Winter Haven, Florida, Cypress Gardens as seen through my 5-year-old eyes in 1944 was very different from the national tourist attraction it later became.

We lived in Auburndale, about 6 miles from the park. The war years were tough: Gas and automobile tires were rationed and scarce, money for family outings even scarcer.

Fortunately, Dick and Julie Pope, the owners of Cypress Gardens, held a Polk County Day once a year, when local residents could get into the beautiful park for free.

For the whole day we forgot our hardships and strolled paths through a fairyland of bougainvilleas, gardenias, azaleas and roses. My favorite was the one I called the bashful plant, though it was probably a touch-me-not (*Mimosa pudica*). The leaves would shrink and close up when I touched them, much as I, a shy girl, felt like doing around people.

I looked forward to seeing the banyan tree, which was planted the year I was born, 1939, and has grown to giant proportions today.

And I stopped at the Wishing Tree, a huge oak damaged in a hurricane, a large limb almost completely torn away. Though partially detached from the mother tree, the limb thrived. A nearby sign promised that if you sat on it and made a wish, your wish would come true. Every year I asked for the same thing—to fly like the birds inhabiting the pines and cypresses in the gardens. My three brothers teased me that it couldn't come true, but the first time I got on a plane, I knew the Wishing Tree had proved them wrong.

CG.17—"Cypress Gardens Aqua Maids"

Cypress Trees and Knees in Florida Cypress Gardens

Daring shows on Lake Eloise made Cypress Gardens the "water-skiing capital of the world."

2023 AQUAPLANING AT THE FLORIDA CYPRESS GARDENS

FROM SWAMP TO SWANK: CYPRESS GARDENS' RISE

IN 1931, DICK AND JULIE POPE BOUGHT several acres of cypress swamp on Lake Eloise in Winter Haven, Florida, for a tourist garden. It took five years to clear the land, dig canals and procure the plants. Cypress Gardens opened Jan. 2, 1936; 182 visitors each paid 25 cents to get in.

The gardens featured more than 30 kinds of palms, 26 varieties of banana trees, 40 varieties of azalea and 30 kinds of camellias. Plants came from Africa, Asia, Oceania and the Americas.

When frost killed vines at the garden gates in 1940, Julie had a staff member in a hooped dress stand nearby to divert visitors' attention. Roaming southern belles were soon added as regular fixtures.

In 1941, when a newspaper printed a picture of the gardens with water-skiers, several servicemen showed up to see the skiing show. There was no such thing at the time, but on the spot, Julie rounded up her kids and friends to put one on. Cypress Gardens has been credited with making water-skiing a craze that lasted well into the 1970s.

A tireless promoter, Dick was known to say to his staff, "I've called the press and told them something big is happening here today. Any ideas?"

The Pope family sold the park in 1985. After several owners, closings and reopenings, the gardens became part of Legoland Florida in 2010, and joined the National Register of Historic Places in 2014.

For 25 cents, visitors could tour the canals in small boats. These rides weren't in our budget, but we enjoyed standing on the wooden bridges as the boats passed below us. I admired the southern belles who roamed the gardens in colorful hooped dresses. At lunch, we'd picnic in the shade.

Between water-ski shows, guests could swim in the lake. There was even a rope tied to one of the cypresses at the shore. What a thrill to swing out and drop in the water. This activity ended when more ski shows were added.

We visited Cypress Gardens on Polk County Day every year until the Popes discontinued the event in the early 1950s. What memories!

BEVERLY SCOTT · AUBURNDALE, FL

The seedling banyan tree planted in 1939 is massive today.

Dan and Karen cut a rug to the Average White Band's "Cut the Cake."

Bumped into the Big Time

It was their chance to get down with disco.

W e had just started dating in 1975 in Kettering, Ohio, when I asked my gal, Karen, if she wanted to take ballroom dancing lessons. She agreed, and it didn't take long before everyone, the instructors in particular, realized Karen was a Dancer with a capital D.

As a teenager she'd danced with a troupe and did solos at fairs around the state. She'd won the talent portions of beauty pageants with her dancing, and choreographed shows across Ohio.

Our studio was participating in a local dance exhibition, which was to feature national ballroom dancing champions and other top-ranked hoofers. One of the instructors approached us about demonstrating the latest disco craze: the bump.

Karen worked me hard for that two-minute routine. Many long hours and aching muscles later, she finally showed me some mercy.

"Well," she said, "I guess that's as good as this is going to get."

Karen and I arrived at the exhibition, which was held at a school gym, to find out that we were to perform first. The funky sounds of the Average White Band's "Cut the Cake" filled the hall, and we bumped and hustled our way through our well-practiced routine. Someone even captured the whole thing on film. The studio paid us a grand sum of $20, which I later joked made us official dancing professionals.

After the show, the visiting dancers and studio instructors had a private party, and to my surprise they invited us. I soon figured out why: All of the pros—the real pros—were itching to dance with Karen. She spent the rest of the night doing tangos, rumbas and waltzes with those guys.

At one point I reminded her to "save the last dance for me."

She did. We've been married for more than 40 years.

DAN GRAHAM · GREENVILLE, SC

STAYIN' ALIVE
AT THE RINK

SEVERAL FRIENDS AND I DECIDED
to go roller-skating one night in the
mid-1970s. Even though I had never
done it, I thought I'd be able to skate,
considering that I'd mastered riding
a unicycle. Once on the rink, though, I
realized quickly that sitting and controlling
one wheel was a breeze compared to
trying to corral four wheels on each foot.
I was courting disaster and I knew it.

Did I mention that this was during the
height of the disco era? The place was
exactly as you might imagine it—a huge
mirror ball hanging at center ceiling,
everyone in gaudy polyester, and the
Bee Gees pumping through the stereo
system at earthquake-level decibels.

For the first hour, I was on my backside
more than I was standing (let alone
skating). So it wasn't only my pride that
was hurting. To top it off, there was a guy
gliding around who thought he was God's
gift to Donna Summer. Not only could he
skate forward *and* backward, he was able
to do so to the rhythm of each song.
I wasn't jealous of his skills, but I was
annoyed that he would point at me and
chuckle every time I fell.

By the last song, this rolling John Travolta
was doing the wheeled version of "The
Hustle" all over the rink. His favorite trick
was to twirl in complete circles while
smiling at me.

Just as he passed me in what I hoped
was the final assault on my battered
self-worth, he suddenly lost his balance.
And, you guessed it, Mr. Disco landed flat
on *his* backside. I saw my chance and took
it. I pointed at the guy, laughed and yelled,
"Thank you, Lord!"

I never attempted to skate again, but
I will always have fond memories of how
that night ended.

ROB MEYERS · GILBERT, AZ

BOOGIE NIGHTS
As teenagers, Danny,
Michael, Kathy and Colleen
would go disco dancing on
Saturday nights in the early
1980s in Willoughby, Ohio.
They kept asking us to go
with them, but we were
reluctant—imagine 40-plus
parents disco dancing with
their kids! One night we
finally gave in and we had
a wonderful time. I still like
disco music and dancing
to this day.
CAROLYN NAGY
AIKEN, SC

EPIC BATTLES
TURNED 'MURRIENT'

WHEN ONE OF US SHOUTED "LET'S PLAY A GAME!"
that usually meant Scrabble. Although one corner of
the burgundy box was held together with yellowed and
peeling tape, it was still our favorite. Our version had
only one true blank tile, as we had etched an A on one
and an L on another in ballpoint pen.

A 14-year span separated the oldest sibling from the
youngest in our family. Any time we played, there was
much cheating, usually in favor of the youngest. "Let me
see your letters," we'd say, and then we'd all brainstorm
on how to get the most points.

We kept our two-letter word list handy, and many of
our X, Y and Z words came from it, including *ex, ax* and
xi. For the Z, if we couldn't find two O's together, we'd
look for an A to spell *za.*

Our best games were late at night, when exhaustion
made us silly. Nonsense words and challenges flew
around the table. One night, my middle brother coined
the word *murrient.* And the argument began.

"That's not a word!"

"Is too!"

"Well, it's not English!"

"Is too!"

"Use it in a sentence!"

"That's not murrient."

We let it stand, though *murrient,* which turned out
to be Latin meaning "squeak like mice," became a family
byword after that. We would use it in a variety of ways
and always with laughter.

One Scrabble game played in the dead of winter
has gone down in family history. My cousin Suzy was
visiting and got pulled into a game that included my
father. Midway through, Dad grew tired of it—he wasn't
winning—so the board "accidentally" flew up from the
table and landed on the floor. Suzy still laughs about it.

Our old version of Scrabble is gone. The new one
is huge and spins on a turntable. But sadly, it gathers
dust as we play lengthy spells of the game Words
with Friends on our smartphones and computers.

At least we can't end our competitions by throwing
the game board anymore.

SANDRA BREWSTER
GLENVILLE, NY

MOM'S THE WORD: SHE'S UNBEATABLE

Mom and Dad—Dorothy and Joseph—
played Scrabble almost every night. Neither
gave the other any special consideration.
Mom was always out to win.

A few years after Dad died, Mom moved
into a senior residence, where she found
three men in her building who would join
her once a week for a game of Scrabble.
She still won most of the time, but the guys
enjoyed her company and the challenge.
KATHY COREY · ST. LOUIS, MO

SCRABBLE SCRIBBLES

Architect Alfred Mosher
Butts invented an early
version of the game in 1933.

·················

It was originally called
Lexiko, a short form
variation of *lexicon,*
meaning "vocabulary"
or "language."

·················

Initially, no game
manufacturers were
interested in it. Butts and
his business partner, James
Brunot, an entrepreneur and
game lover, began producing
the game themselves and
called it Scrabble, which
means "to grope frantically."

·················

About 33 percent
of American homes own
a Scrabble game.

·················

Competitors in the
North American Scrabble
Players Association's annual
championship tournament
use tiles that are smooth
on both sides so they can't
tell the blanks from the
lettered tiles when selecting
them from the bag.

Scrabble comes in 29 languages.
More than 150 million games
have been sold worldwide.

Box Supper Bombshell

By auction time, everyone knew the secret of the colored ribbons.

Box supper weather occurs in the late fall before winter starts. Usually by this time of year there has already been a killing frost, so the trees are enriched by beautiful colors. The watermelons and gardens are long gone, and pumpkins can be seen among the turnip patches, not yet harvested. Soon the persimmons will start ripening.

During this special time of year, most schools in the county where I grew up would have a box supper. This was a favorite means of raising money. The young ladies of the school district decorated boxes and filled them with homemade cookies, pies, sandwiches and even full meals. Inside each box, the woman would include a piece of paper with her name. At a specified time they would secretly deliver the boxes to the school so no one would guess whose box belonged to whom.

The boxes were auctioned to raise money. Naturally, each married man knew which was his wife's and was expected to bid on it. The real competition was among unmarried men, who would bid on the most attractive box and share the contents with the young lady who had brought it. Sometimes, real dates would ensue.

One of my teachers, Anne, had a boyfriend, Fred. The day of the box supper, my friends Bill and John overheard a conversation between the couple. Anne told Fred that her box would have a red, white and blue ribbon on top of the white handle. He couldn't miss it.

Bill and John immediately spread the news to the other young men in town who were interested in bidding for Miss Anne's box supper. But they didn't stop there. They also persuaded several young ladies to decorate their boxes the same way. Now the stage was set.

Bidding at the box supper that night was frantic. Six similarly decorated boxes were auctioned off, and Fred was outbid on all but the last one. When the final box with the pretty patriotic ribbon came up, Fred bid 25 cents and won, because everyone else had spent their money on the counterfeit boxes. He was lucky enough to get the one made by Miss Anne. Bill and John, watching from the sidelines, laughed hysterically.

For the first time, a teacher's box sold for the low bid. Even so, the evening raised more money than anyone could remember. It was a success, and everyone found their box supper cooks and enjoyed the evening.

Box suppers were a highlight in our rural community. They were an inexpensive kind of entertainment that gave us a reason to get together, taking our minds off the problems of making a living.

NEAL MURPHY · SAN AUGUSTINE, TX

BUSIEST ROOM IN THE HOUSE

Bathrooms have received some colorful attention over the years. Do you remember these items?

1972 »

Cloud Variations

This eye-catching Sears ad ran a full page in *Better Homes and Gardens*. It describes a dizzying number of possible combinations—ovals, oblongs, rounds and contours, with or without fringe, and in 13 colors. Who knew choosing a humble bath rug could be so complicated?

« 1956

Pretty in Pastel

Soft-Weve was among the first to make toilet paper in the pinks, blues, greens and yellows of midcentury bathrooms—because who wouldn't want to match the paper to the fixtures? Colored toilet paper was popular into the 1970s, when sales waned amid warnings that it could cause skin irritation and that the dyes were damaging the environment.

Marching to the Same Beat

Music strikes a major chord for everyone in the family.

M y family's symphony of life started before I was born. When my dad, Edward Kulesza, was in high school, he loved to listen to his neighbor, a professional saxophone player, practicing his music. Dad was so mesmerized by it that he decided to try to play sax in his school band. Unfortunately, the only horn available was a trombone. Dad gave it his best, but he had to quit at 16 when he left school to get a job to help support his family.

Flash forward a few decades to when I played alto saxophone at Royal Oak Dondero High School at the urging of—you guessed it—my dad. He strongly encouraged me to follow a musical path and was wonderful about my practice sessions, even though he needed to rest in the evenings before he went to his second job. If Mom would start to chastise me, Dad would say, "No, I want to hear her play as I go to sleep."

Dondero High used to host a yearly cavalcade of area high school marching bands. At one of these events my friends and I were walking by the field stands when we noticed a large group of people huddled near something on the ground. It seemed that someone had dropped a trumpet, and the horn was down for the count. We all had a good laugh about the idiot who'd fumbled his instrument.

Well, it gets even funnier: I married that idiot. Brian and I met in college, and it was only when we were dating seriously that I found out he was the poor guy who'd dropped his trumpet at the high school band event. (His parents later had the horn repaired.)

Brian and I discovered another surprising connection. Remember the saxophone-playing neighbor who had inspired my father, who in turn encouraged me to pursue music? That was George Lupanoff, my husband's grandfather.

Now our song plays on through our daughter Kim Pullen, a percussionist with a degree in music performance. She went to Brian's high school. At a special reunion event, all three of us marched and played with the band on the football field. It was a dream come true for this old band geek.

CHERYL KULESZA BURNEY
ROYAL OAK, MI

Clockwise from top left: Cheryl and her alto sax in her sophomore year, 1979-'80; Cheryl's dad, Edward, who passed on his love of music; Brian and his ill-fated trumpet, years before its downfall; the Burneys' daughter Kim, who earned a bachelor's degree in music performance.

TOE TAPPING

SKIRTING AROUND THE ISSUE

When I started cello in the fifth grade in 1962, girls had to wear only skirts or dresses to school. But I had special permission to wear pants on the days that I had lessons or orchestra practice.
GENEVE HARRIS · ROCKFORD, IL

MOTHER-DAUGHTER DUET

At age 10 in 1958, I started taking lessons on a 12-button bass accordion in our small city of Fremont, Nebraska. My mother basically learned along with me and we both became quite good. We'd play during Saturday night get-togethers. The adults tipped their whiskey highballs and glasses of beer while tapping their feet to our rendition of "Beer Barrel Polka."
ANAMARIE WOSTRCHILL · CENTENNIAL, CO

TWO CAN PLAY THAT TUNE

My dad was a big fan of accordionist Myron Floren on *The Lawrence Welk Show*. Before I knew it, he'd signed up my sister and me for lessons, and within a year, we were performing as a duet at business luncheons, club meetings and retirement homes. In this picture from 1955, I'm 8 (left) and Karen is 6.
KRISTINE ANN SHELL · REDLANDS, CA

PREACHING TO THE CHOIR

My daddy was a preacher and told my music teachers that he wanted me to learn "so one day she can play for church." I took piano in Texas until we moved to Virginia, where he bought me a red accordion and I began lessons. More than 65 years later I still have that accordion and still play it. It has my name on it, though somehow they managed to misspell it as "Sissie."

MARY "SISSY" SOMMERS STOVALL
CLEVELAND, TN

DRESS REHEARSAL

This is my father-in-law, John Ashton, in 1918, at age 8, all spruced up for his violin recital. We enjoyed his playing for years at family gatherings.

PHILIP ELDER · WEST PALM BEACH, FL

PICK OF THE PACK

Dad signed me up for a steel-guitar class in Joplin, Missouri, in 1949, when I was 9. As a top student, I was featured on a Sunday radio promotion. In high school in Memphis, Tennessee, I played in a country band with classmate Larry "Red" Manuel, who was later inducted into the Rockabilly Hall of Fame.

ROLAND SNEED
BLUE SPRINGS, MO

ON YOUR MARK, GET SET, GO!

NO ENGINE NEEDED

The Scouts sponsored the 1946 Soap Box Derby in Susanville, California.
Boys prep to race down Main Street.
PHOTO COURTESY OF LASSEN HISTORICAL SOCIETY • SUSANVILLE, CA

DAD-MADE MOTOR CAR

My husband, William, couldn't throw
anything away. In 1959, using a motor
and wheels from a discarded lawn
mower, he built a go-kart for our
kids, Bill and Shirley. They drove the
motor car around the supermarket
parking lot.

MARTHA MAHON • TRENTON, NJ

ONE PUSH REQUIRED

We called it a pushie, and in 1954 my brother Dennis,
standing, and I raced it down the hilly streets of our
Pottstown, Pennsylvania, neighborhood. Ours was always
the fastest. My grandfather was caretaker for a local estate,
and the owner gave him a set of professional-looking Soap
Box Derby wheels with ball bearings and iron axles. We
rigged a steering wheel to a rope to control the front tires.
ALAN KLINE • POTTSTOWN, PA

COURTING FAVORS

Getting ready for the Soap Box Derby in Coshocton, Ohio, when I was 12, gave me the butterflies. My dad and I used old crates from my uncle's appliance store to build the car. I won the first heat but lost the second. My youngest daughter and her husband now display the car in their pole barn.

RICHARD STAFFORD
FRAZEYSBURG, OH

ALL-AROUND HANDYMAN

My father could fix, build and drive anything. He built his first car at 15. Next he built a dragster, then dune buggies. To me he was Superman. I was one lucky girl to have David Hutchinson as my dad!

SUSAN HUTCHINSON
SAN DIMAS, CA

WINTER GAMES

SLEDDING SQUAD

Our dad, Frank Lyons, would load our station wagon with sleds and kids and off we'd go. Here we are at Bradys Run Park in Beaver Falls, Pennsylvania, in January 1966: my sister Susan, my brother Paul, neighbors Pete and David Matich, me and my brother Tim.

JUDY THARP · MONACA, PA

D-I-Y SLED

Willamette Valley in Oregon has a mild climate with little snow. But on this winter day in 1982, Mother Nature dropped over 6 inches in our area. Bob, my husband, tied a rope to a Hunt's box and pulled our 2-year-old son Cooper up and down the street. Then they came home for some hot cocoa.

ROBBIE WRIGHT
EUGENE, OR

My uncle Merle was an avid skier and an amateur
photographer. I found this picture of skiers dressed as
snow bunnies in his collection of slides, which record
more than 20 years of his skiing travels.

CHUCK BELLING · MADISON, WI

Skiing Mount Tacoma, the locals' name for Mount Rainier, became Ruth's winter tradition.

First-Time Ski Instructions

Keep it simple and you'll survive.

Hot, spicy chili beans filled my gallon thermos. In the late '30s, I was dressed in layers of wool, with mittens, cap and borrowed boots. It was 6 a.m. and I was ready.

My church buddies picked me up and we headed to Mount Rainier. After a few hours of chatter, we arrived and parked Big Joe's 1930 Buick near the ranger station.

"Leave all food and changes of clothing in the car," Joe said as he locked the vehicle.

We hiked up a narrow, snow-dusted trail to Paradise Inn, where we ate lunch. Afterward, we headed to the top of the ski slope. Big Joe was experienced, so he gave me a crash course while attaching skis to my boots and handing me the poles.

"But I've never skied," I admitted. He looked at me and said, "You step, then you glide. Step. Glide. Piece o' cake." Then he disappeared with the others down the snow-covered slopes.

My friend Mayo confessed that she couldn't ski either. "We'll stick together," I assured her as we both started down the hill.

Mayo took a few steps and glides before yelling, "Hey, we're doing better than I thought."

That was her mistake, as she then tumbled into an acrobatic spill. After unlatching her skis, she stood in snow up to her knees, slung her skis over her shoulder, and proceeded to take giant steps toward me using her poles for balance.

"I'll slow down and wait for you," I said as I stepped and glided past her. My mistake. I lost my balance and did a giant flip-flop, then landed on my back looking up at my skis, with my poles on tree limbs. It took me several minutes to unravel and stand up.

Now we both were toting our skis on our shoulders, goose-stepping in the waist-high powdery snow. At this point, we were a little giddy with fear and frenzy, trying to be brave. All we cared about was surviving the cold terrain.

By the time we got back to the car, the sunlight had paled and it was dusk. A uniformed ranger spotted us with his flashlight, and he and Joe brought us dry jackets.

Everyone else was gathered around a bonfire, staying warm and waiting for us. They all applauded when we arrived.

Sitting next to Joe on the drive home, he gave me a squeeze and whispered, "Told you it'd be a piece o' cake."

RUTH J. ANDERSON
PORT ANGELES, WA

All Polished Up

For my first recital, when I was 7, my Grandma Nana took
me to get a manicure. If the guys in the neighborhood
had seen my nail polish, I would've been in for a fight.

MICHAEL G. KADLUBOWSKI · LOMBARD, IL

CHAPTER 5

AT WORK

Read touching accounts of hard work
and tenacity, the kind that gets us all
through tough times.

Folded Pairs

During the first half of the 20th century, the Phoenix Hosiery Co. was a mainstay in downtown Milwaukee, Wisconsin. Working in one of the company's six plants, these factory workers folded and packed the product for seamless shipping nationwide.

The Phoenix Hosiery Co. owned several buildings in Milwaukee's Third Ward district.

Stocking Stuffers

A once-thriving hosiery factory met a fickle fate.

S oon after moving from Beloit, Wisconsin, to Milwaukee in 1968, my career path took a couple of interesting turns. I was intrigued by airplanes and started working in the data processing and reservation departments for North Central Airlines. But when the company consolidated functions in its Minneapolis headquarters, I decided to stay in Milwaukee and look for something else.

I eventually found work in the distribution center at Kayser-Roth Corp., housed in the Phoenix Building near the heart of downtown Milwaukee. Kayser-Roth had purchased the Phoenix Hosiery Co., and by the late 1960s, all production had moved to North Carolina. What remained in Milwaukee

PHOENIX HOSIERY CO.

Based in Milwaukee, Wisconsin, from 1897 to 1959

....

Barbara Newberry, a performer with the Ziegfeld Follies, modeled Phoenix hosiery in a 1929 ad campaign

....

Sold to Kayser-Roth Corp. in 1959

....

Production moved to North Carolina, but warehousing and shipping remained in Milwaukee until 1973

were the warehouse and shipping functions. I ran the warehouse and managed the office personnel; I'm a people person, so it was a great fit.

But fashions changed and so did the hosiery business. As women began to wear more pantsuits and slacks, stockings and pantyhose went out of style.

I worked there until the mid-'70s, when the company decided to close the office and move all remaining functions to North Carolina.

While clearing everything out, I discovered a discarded box that was filled with newsletters and these company photos from the 1930s and '40s. It was fun to look back at the early, flourishing days of this business.

GARY JENSEN
OCONOMOWOC, WI

WORKERS TAKE PRIDE IN FANCY FOOTWORK

1. High standards at the Phoenix Hosiery plant required eight major inspections. **2.** Winding thread from spools to cones was called coning and made the knitting process smoother. **3.** Menders worked with their hands instead of machines. **4.** Stockings, shaped on boards after dyeing, moved along an assembly line into dryers.

Sisters Bring the Heat

One specific skill set gave them
steady work during WWII.

A t a family reunion in 2016, my cousin's wife insisted that I tell the story of my mom and her two sisters. I had the photos, along with other documents my mom had saved in a scrapbook. One photo shows my mom, Elaine Carlson, and her sisters Ruth and June wearing welding masks, jackets and gloves during World War II. The trio moved from Minnesota to Indiana in 1941 and worked as welders until the war ended in 1945.

Here's how they landed in Indiana.

My mom's dad, Gustaf, was a Swedish immigrant who became a tenant farmer in northwest Minnesota. He married Clara and the couple settled in Red Lake, where they raised eight children—four boys and four girls.

My mom was born in 1921 and graduated from Kelliher High School in 1939. Afterward she went to work in the hospital kitchen in Duluth where her older sister Ruth was studying to be a nurse. There she met my dad, Lester Pelander, while he was recuperating from a skiing accident.

Three sisters—from left, June, Elaine and Ruth Carlson—shared a room for $8 a month.

When war was declared on Dec. 8, 1941, everything changed. Dad, who had been a Duluth-area skier, joined the military and was sent to the Aleutian Islands as a ski instructor. My mom and Ruth were joined by their youngest sister, June, who had graduated by that time. The three women attended Zenith vocational training school to learn welding. Once they finished, they were approached by a recruiter, Joe Morris, from Jeffersonville Boat & Machine Co. in Jeffersonville, Indiana. He interviewed them at noon, and that night they were on a train to Indiana.

My mom and my aunts were among the many women who went to work in factories to support the war effort. All three worked in a factory welding LSTs (an acronym for Landing Ship, Tank), which were used to transport troops, vehicles and supplies during missions to France, Sicily and Italy, and in the Pacific. They roomed together at a boarding house in New Albany, Indiana. When the war ended in 1945, all three returned to Minnesota to rekindle relationships and start new lives.

ROD PELANDER
FERGUSON, MO

When war was declared on Dec. 8, 1941, everything changed.

Learning the ropes, youngest sister June kneels while Ruth, left, and Elaine give her pointers.

First Impressions Count

Your past is a good indication of what you'll do in the future.

G etting my first official job when I turned 16 in 1959 taught me valuable skills. John Monsour, a pleasant, hardworking man and the owner of Penhurst Fruit Market, wanted me to work for him. My mother and grandmother were longtime shoppers and he admired their reputations.

He hired me to work after school and all day on Saturdays. My starting wage was 30 cents an hour, but Mr. Monsour told me that once I learned the job and became more valuable, he would increase my pay to 85 cents an hour, close to minimum wage.

When I started, I needed to overcome my shyness. I learned to greet customers, establish a rapport with them, and earn their trust so that they would return. My duties expanded, and soon I was waiting on customers, displaying and watering the produce, washing windows, raking sawdust from the floors, and delivering groceries.

I worked hard and it paid off. The job kept me away from the neighborhood mischief. And at the beginning of my senior year in high school, Mr. Monsour raised my wage to $1 an hour. He told me not to tell the other workers. Mum was the word; I wasn't going to mess up my good thing!

My earnings enabled me to buy school clothes, and I no longer had to think about

Harry's wages allowed him to dress well while attending Westinghouse High School in Pittsburgh in 1961.

dropping out because I didn't have the right things to wear. I became more confident, gregarious and self-sufficient. I paid my way and felt useful and important to my family.

After high school, I worked through college and earned an MBA in finance. I was offered a dream job in Washington, D.C., doing international banking, a position requiring a security clearance. I got the job.

Later, while visiting my family in Pittsburgh, I stopped at the fruit market to say hello to Mr. Monsour. He joked that I had brought the feds down on him.

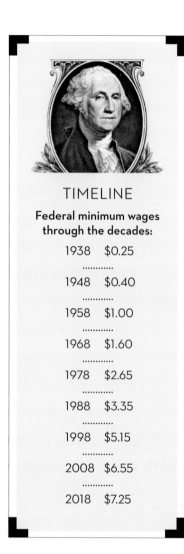

TIMELINE

Federal minimum wages through the decades:

1938	$0.25
1948	$0.40
1958	$1.00
1968	$1.60
1978	$2.65
1988	$3.35
1998	$5.15
2008	$6.55
2018	$7.25

I thought: *Wow, they went to my high school employer to ask about me and my work performance.*

My mother always told me: "Harry, every job you do is important, so always do your best." I learned early the wisdom of those words.

HARRY JAMES FORD
PITTSBURGH, PA

Rosario (far left) and brothers Giuseppe and Andrea staff the barbershop they built in Gary, Indiana.

With Only $2 in His Pocket

He built a life doing what he knew best.

M y husband, Rosario Cammarata, arrived in the United States from Sicily in 1958 with his mother, two brothers and $2 his father had given him. The family settled in Gary, Indiana, but Rosario was forced to quit high school and find a job to support his mother and siblings. He was considered a master barber back in Sicily, so he got a job at a barbershop.

After two years, his boss asked if he wanted to buy the shop. Because Rosario had saved his money, he was able to buy his first barbershop in downtown Gary at 18.

In 1966, he built a barbershop and an adjoining building in a Gary neighborhood with help from his brothers. We got married that year and went to Italy for two months. When we returned, Rosario started Gary's first soccer league for adults.

By 1977, we had three sons and moved to Lake Havasu City, Arizona, where Rosario opened a one-man shop in a mall. He worked

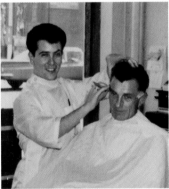

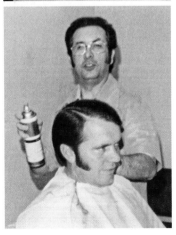

Rosario cuts hair in his shops in downtown Gary, Indiana (top), and in Lake Havasu City, Arizona.

for almost 10 years there. Once again, Rosario's love of soccer prompted him to start the city's first soccer league.

The family moved to Phoenix in 1987 and Rosario worked for Smitty's Barbershop for a short while before buying his own shop in Mesa. After a few years his brothers joined him again and eventually he bought another shop in Scottsdale. Rosario ran one shop and one of his brothers ran the other. By April 2016, the brothers had sold both shops.

Rosario now has dementia and no longer runs a barbershop, but he can still cut hair. He often gets together with former employees to trade stories about the old shop and the great times they had.

So at 16, Rosario came to America with only $2 in his pocket, yet went on to make an amazing life for himself and his entire family.

CAROL CAMMARATA
CAVE CREEK, AZ

Service Came with a Smile

Her positive attitude earned praise.

Times were tough in the 1930s. After my mother, Bertha May Royston Crossley, lost her dad when she was 11, staying in school became a luxury. So she quit school when she was old enough and went to work. She was hired at a local sewing factory in Shrewsbury, Pennsylvania, despite having only an eighth-grade education.

While at the factory, she met my dad, Thomas Crossley, and they were soon married. Afterward, she stayed home with her three children until the youngest, me, was in the third grade. Then she decided it was time she went out and got a job.

Lacking education and experience, she was hired by Sears, Roebuck and Co. for an entry-level job in the garden shop. But when an office job opened, she applied and was put in charge of the routing desk.

School let out earlier than Mom got off work, so on many days I would meet her at Sears. I had a grand time waiting at her office. On occasion, Mom would hand me a ticket to file in the cubby next to her desk. I felt so important, so sure that I was helping her. Then she would give me a quarter and I would buy a hot dog from the deli downstairs.

A big part of her job was talking to customers on the phone and letting them know when their purchases would be delivered. Sometimes the customers became impatient because deliveries were late or something arrived damaged. But no matter the mood of the customer, Mom always spoke quietly and calmed many potential storms for Sears.

At the end of each day, she walked around the store to pick up order tickets, and took them back to her desk to schedule the deliveries.

I was so proud of my mom. She dressed professionally and always wore a smile. Everyone had friendly words for her as she passed their stations. And she took every chance to greet her fellow workers as she walked past.

Those were good times, and I have warm memories of spending so many afternoons with my mom. I acquired my good work ethic from watching and following her example.

E.M. "COOKIE" MILLER
YELM, WA

SEARS TIMELINE

1886
Richard W. Sears launches a mail-order business selling watches.

· · · · · · · · · · · · · · · ·

1887
Alvah C. Roebuck joins Sears as a watch repairer.

· · · · · · · · · · · · · · · ·

1893
The partners officially call their company Sears, Roebuck and Co.

· · · · · · · · · · · · · · · ·

1924
Sears launches a Chicago, Illinois, radio station, eventually settling on call letters WLS (World's Largest Store).

· · · · · · · · · · · · · · · ·

1925
The first retail Sears store opens in Chicago.

· · · · · · · · · · · · · · · ·

1933
Sears issues its first Christmas Book, renamed the Wish Book in 1968.

· · · · · · · · · · · · · · · ·

2005
Major merger: Sears and Kmart.

Five years before she retired at Sears, Bertha got written up on the board—big kudos from her boss.

This Goede family photo was taken in 1960 at Mader's restaurant in Milwaukee, Wisconsin. From left: Julie, Sandy, Olivia, Paul, Diane and Steve.

Teach a Man to Cook

While others ate his food, Dad dreamed up new dishes.

Both of my parents worked in the 1950s while my siblings and I were growing up in our small town in southern Wisconsin. My mother, Olivia Goede, was a registered nurse at Edgerton Hospital, and my father, Paul, was a chef. In the early 1960s, he worked at Mader's, a top German restaurant in Milwaukee, Wisconsin.

Like most chefs, he was always experimenting with different food combinations and new recipes. He finished third in 1960 in a national sandwich contest with his creation "Dreamy, Creamy, Nutty Tuna." My sister Sandy came up with the name.

His winnings included a trip to New York City. After airfare and the tailored suit my father purchased for the trip, my mother guessed he barely broke even. Regardless, the whole family was proud of Dad and the work he did.

The tuna sandwich was not his only prizewinning recipe. He won a dessert contest sponsored by the Door County (Wisconsin) Cherry Association, and that earned the family a week's stay at the Anderson Hotel in Ephraim in Door County.

Then in the 1980s, when he was food service director for the University of Wisconsin-Stout, Dad won a contest sponsored by the Citrus Growers of Florida for his recipe for *boeuf en croute* with orange sauce.

My father often did catering jobs that included the whole family, and my mom worked full time and raised four kids. We were so lucky to have parents who encouraged creativity and instilled a strong work ethic in all of us.

DIANE GOEDE LUTZ
BEAVER DAM, WI

Farm Futures

Rural life replaced city style.

Stella worked as a deputy auditor but left to marry. She kept the books on the family farm for more than 70 years.

Seventy-six years ago, I was in my early 20s and I was ready to conquer the working world.

I lived at Lorraine Apartments in Spencer, Iowa, near the old library. My roommate, Leone Shaeffer, and I were literal roommates: Instead of an apartment, we shared the apartment owner's bedroom on the first floor, while the owner slept on a cot in her living room. We also shared her bathroom. Breakfast was included in our modest rent. Our landlady didn't charge much, which was good because we didn't get paid a lot.

Weekdays, I walked several blocks daily to the Clay County Courthouse, where I worked as a deputy auditor. After work, I would meet Leone, who worked at the American Automobile Association office. We often stopped by The Woman Shop on the east side of Main Street as we walked home.

We couldn't afford the latest stylish clothes, but we loved to browse. Even though we didn't wear hats, we liked to try them on. And when we had money, we'd buy a new dress for work.

This was during World War II, when women's nylon stockings were scarce and expensive. If we didn't have nylons, we went barelegged. Sometimes a clerk at The Woman Shop would save a light beige pair of stockings with a seam up the back behind the counter for us.

The shop owner, Mr. Dvergsten (known as Mr. D),

often rang up the sales himself. We didn't have credit cards, so Mr. D would write up a sales slip with a carbon copy and stamp it "ON APPROVAL" in big letters. No money changed hands. In a day or two, I would either return the item or pay him.

My job at the courthouse was a good position in the early 1940s, but I left when I got married. Looking back, my husband, Donald, and I could have used the extra money. But things were different then,

and I happily became one of the many stay-at-home wives of my generation.

My friends at the courthouse sent me off to my new married life with an old-fashioned shivaree. They came out to our farm honking horns and clanging on pans.

Donald and I were married for 71 years. I guess you could say it was another wise career choice.

STELLA KING WILSON
DICKENS, IA

The Stroudsmoor had room for up to 160 guests, most of them from New York City and Long Island. Fred worked 12-hour days, seven days a week, as part of the hotel waitstaff.

YOUR REFRESHMENT, SIR AND MADAM

SUMMERS DURING MY JUNIOR AND SENIOR years of high school in 1949 and '50 were spent working as a bellhop at the Stroudsmoor Hotel in Stroudsburg, Pennsylvania. I was only 16, and they would have preferred someone of college age, but they needed someone *now*. Plus I was tall for my age, and they must have believed I could carry luggage without difficulty. In addition to carting suitcases in and out, I delivered beverages to various locations on the property—to the rooms, tennis court, swimming pool or recreation area. I got room and board, plus $5 a week; tips averaged $60 to $65 a week.

Working those two summers gave me the people skills that proved invaluable throughout my career as a teacher, principal and eventually superintendent of schools.

FRED SERFASS
POTTSTOWN, PA

SMALL TALK WITH FRIENDS

A TALKER BY NATURE, MY MOTHER, Barbara Fleece, worked as a switchboard operator for Michigan Bell Telephone Co. in 1951 when she was 18. It was her first real job and she won an award for her outstanding work performance.

While there, my mom worked alongside one of her dearest lifelong friends, Jean Bradford. Often between customer service calls during their work shifts, they would connect to each other's control-board consoles and chat. Their supervisor eventually caught on to their ruse and split them up. As a result, Jean was assigned to a different area servicing long-distance calls, and Mom continued to work on local calls.

STAN FLEECE
TRAVERSE CITY, MI

Connecting calls for customers was Barbara's job, but it also gave her an outlet for her caring spirit.

Try the Meatball Sandwich

Mom knew a thing or two about Italian cooking.

Like all Italian mothers, my mom, Mae DiMarco, made the best spaghetti sauce in the world. But unlike the other moms, her sauce went public in front of Hollywood stars.

My dad had received two valuable food-stand franchises for the Los Angeles County Fair when it reopened in 1948. Prior to that, the location had served as a military camp and prisoner of war center during and after World War II. Dad decided to serve traditional hamburgers and hot dogs in one of the stands. In the other, he took a chance by serving lesser-known items—Italian sandwiches. One of them was a meatball sandwich dipped in pasta sauce. And whose meatballs and sauce would be better to serve than my mother's?

The sandwiches consisted of three meatballs smothered in Mom's delicious sauce and served on a tasty French roll. They were a big hit at the fair, the second-largest in the country. But in 1950, the sandwiches underwent a stiff taste test.

Ezio Pinza, the famous Metropolitan Opera basso, had undertaken the male lead in *South Pacific* when it opened on Broadway in 1949. The show, co-starring Mary Martin, became a megahit and introduced such songs as "Some Enchanted Evening" and "Bali Ha'i." After winning a Tony Award at 57, Pinza became a household name.

While in Hollywood to fulfill a movie contract with MGM, Pinza visited the fair. When my mother spotted him eyeing our sign with skepticism, she quickly made him a meatball sandwich free of charge. He took it and then disappeared.

A short while later, he returned, this time with an entourage of almost a dozen people. My mom asked, *"Ti è piaciuto?"* (Did you like it?)

A broad smile came over Pinza's face as he replied, *"Deliziosa!"*

He ordered a dozen sandwiches on the spot and later came back for more. It certainly was a fine endorsement but not a surprise for those of us who had enjoyed Mom's cooking for years.

How could Ezio Pinza not have liked her sauce? It was the best.

TONY DiMARCO
LOS ANGELES, CA

Tony worked the food stand where his mom and dad introduced Italian sandwiches to fairgoers.

FUN FACTS

Ezio Pinza could not read music; he memorized every song.

....

Pinza spent 22 years with the New York Metropolitan Opera.

....

During a scene in the 1980 film *The Blues Brothers*, Pinza's voice is heard singing *"Anema e core."*

HOOFING IT ON THE BALLROOM FLOOR

BEING A TEENAGER DURING World War II in Hebron, a small town in central Ohio, presented a special employment opportunity for me and my contemporaries. Everyone just a few years older than us was either inducted into the service or employed by one of the defense plants that had cropped up. As a result, jobs not previously available to kids were ours for the asking.

Nearby was an amusement park called Buckeye Lake, also known as the Playground of Ohio. The park had a variety of rides, concessions, games and eateries, as well as a skating rink and two dance halls. The plethora of jobs there was amazing, and the laws covering child labor were much more relaxed than they are today.

I began working in 1944, when I was 14, at a dance hall, the Crystal Ballroom.

As the dance floor manager, I supervised 10 ticket takers, mopped and treated the dance floor with cornmeal and shaved paraffin, and set up music stands and microphones.

A house band was booked for the entire summer. However, big-name bands such as the Dorsey brothers, Benny Goodman, Harry James, Charlie Barnet, Gene Krupa and even Spike Jones made occasional appearances. We used the dime-a-dance ticket system with the house band. With big names, however, we charged a general admission fee but the dancing was free.

After each dance number, I hustled everyone off the dance floor. I also made sure that no one was inebriated and that the dancing didn't get excessively vigorous. The jitterbug was big and at times people overdid it.

We worked seven days a week from 7 p.m. until close at 1 a.m. Then we walked 2 miles home along a busy highway full of drivers who had been doing their fair share of drinking that night. I worked there for three years before joining the Navy when I turned 17.

There is no way parents would allow kids to do this today.

JOHN COOPERIDER
HOOKSETT, NH

In the late '20s, Jack worked on a crew installing power lines in Ohio. Steady work on utility crews meant Jack moved his family around a lot.

RETURNING THE FAVOR

My father, Jack LeRoy Unland, found work during the late 1920s and '30s throughout Ohio and Illinois installing telephone and electric lines, and farming during the Depression. In all those years I don't remember Dad ever saying anything derogatory about anyone. Nor did he and my mother argue in front of us kids. Dad was the kind of guy who picked up hitchhikers from Ohio State University, because other people had helped him when he needed a hand.

MAXINE THOMPSON · BRADENTON, FL

VINTAGE ADS · VINTAGE ADS

PASTEL REVOLUTION

Earl S. Tupper's "plastic of the future" and Brownie Wise's genius for selling it launched a marvel of the 20th century: Tupperware. The product transformed the American household, gave women new earning power and paved the way for today's shop-at-home lifestyle.

Kitchen Innovation
Early versions of Tupper's line were all white and sold at department stores. But sales were slow until a woman named Brownie Wise threw a party to show how bowls could actually bounce. The Plastic of the Future, as it was called, was trademarked as Poly-T by Tupper Plastics. It was marketed as being flexible and featherweight.

1970s

Rainbow of Food Storage

Burnt orange, avocado and gold were the dominant
Tupperware colors in the 1970s.

ALL IN A DAY'S WORK

My mom worked at the Starlite Dude Ranch Drive-In, Maryville, Missouri, in '64. She loved the job but hated wearing a cowboy hat because it messed up her beehive hairdo.

SHANNON SCHNEIDER
WAMEGO, KS

PICK A PECK

I was 15 when I got my first job in 1954 working at Sunnyside Farm Products in Affton, Missouri, near St. Louis. The farm stand's owner, Ray Knierim, employed teenage clerks and paid them 50 cents an hour. We worked so many hours, sometimes I made as much as my mom, who worked at the local bank.

JIM EYDMANN · GRANITE CITY, IL

ENOUGH FOR EVERYONE

Prep cooks in the cafeteria of Cockrill Elementary School in Nashville, Tennessee, ready food trays in this photo from the early 1940s. My mother-in-law, Jerdie Toler Garland (far right), worked there. Schools and church basements were often used as sites for fundraising meals. At that time, volunteers converged on the kitchens to whip up mass quantities of food.

MARIE MURPHY GARLAND · NASHVILLE, TN

—❝—

While I was home from college, my summer job in 1969 was driving my scooter through neighborhoods in Rochester, New York, selling Skippy ice cream. I rang the bells and kids raced out to greet me.

DAVE SKIRVIN · INDIANAPOLIS, IN

After a bust, Charles Campbell, second from right, hides his .38-caliber revolver under his suit jacket after finding an illegal still in South Dakota.

Memories of an ATF Agent

Upholding the law before and after Prohibition.

M y father, Charles E. Campbell, joined the Bureau of Prohibition, forerunner to the Bureau of Alcohol, Tobacco, Firearms and Explosives, in 1920 as a prohibition agent. After the 18th Amendment passed in 1919, the production and sale of alcohol was outlawed. The Volstead Act gave the federal agency power to enforce the law.

Although not a member of Eliot Ness' fabled Untouchables in Chicago, Illinois, my father nonetheless was in the second group of agents joining the agency, stationed in both Chicago and Omaha, Nebraska.

More than a decade later, after Prohibition was repealed, he continued as an agent stationed in Rapid City, South Dakota, sharing an office and a secretary with an FBI agent. In the late '40s and '50s, the crimes that justified federal intervention in western South Dakota included possessing automatic firearms, operating stills, and smuggling alcohol into the country without paying federal taxes.

One of the many stories my dad told involved a group of enterprising criminals who tried to sell Scotch whisky smuggled from Canada into Rapid City without paying the federal tax. With the help of an informant, Agent Campbell busted the criminals.

For his length of service and the outstanding number of arrests he made, my father received the Albert Gallatin Award. His name is displayed in the foyer of the U.S. Treasury Department in Washington, D.C.

CAL CAMPBELL
VENICE, FL

Homefront Volunteers

In 1943, women in white met monthly in the basement of the United Reformed Church of Williamsbridge Road in the Bronx, New York, to roll bandages for medical hospitals overseas. My mother-in-law, Anna Ahders, second row, second from right, volunteered for the cause.

JOAN AHDERS · NEW HARTFORD, NY

CHAPTER 6

OUR
HEROES

They gave of themselves for freedom.
We honor their personal stories and
those from family members here.

They Made It Their Own

"Home is where you dig it" reads the sign over the fighting bunker
of privates from the 1st Battalion, 7th Marine Regiment,
during Operation Worth in Vietnam, March 1968.

Operation Big Switch

A soldier recounts the emotional exchange of prisoners at the close of the Korean War.

With the signing of the armistice that ended the Korean War on July 27, 1953, I was sent to assist with the exchange of prisoners known as Operation Big Switch. Few today know about this phase of the conflict, but it affected some 87,000 troops on both sides.

Operation Big Switch involved the repatriation of soldiers and civilians who'd been taken captive during the fighting, including more than 3,000 Americans.

A few months before Big Switch began, a smaller swap of sick and wounded prisoners called Operation Little Switch occurred at the capital, Seoul. I had watched as helicopters, each with four wounded returnees, touched down in a clearing among Seoul's bombed-out buildings. Hundreds of Koreans lined the perimeter of the landing circle, with more seated on the surrounding rubble, all desperate to see a father, husband or son among the wounded.

The crowd was silent, the only sound coming from the rhythmic *swish* of the helicopter rotors. As soon as the aircraft grazed the ground, the crowd burst into a loud, brief cheer before falling

Left, wounded
POWs land in
Seoul, South Korea.
Cpl. Fred Benton,
below, witnessed
the repatriation of
Korean War prisoners.

silent again. Nothing I ever
witnessed touched me as
much as that.

Later, I reported to the
55th Replacement Company
in the South Korean port city
of Inchon, a repatriation site
for Operation Big Switch.
Helicopters were already
delivering our returning soldiers.
My heart beat fast as I saw the
aircraft land, wait just long
enough to allow passengers to
disembark, then quickly take
off again to retrieve more POWs.

I saw five repatriates exit a
helicopter, duck to avoid the

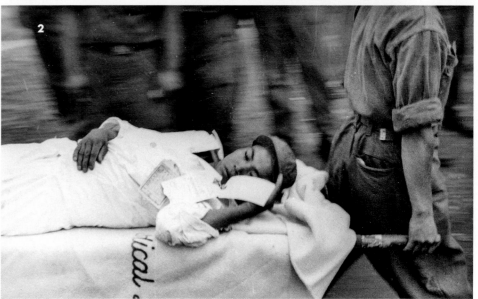

1. Freed prisoners hurry to get off the helicopter at Inchon, South Korea.
2. A wounded POW is carried off the chopper in Seoul.
3. Hundreds wait in silence during Operation Little Switch in Seoul, anxious to see a loved one.
4. A sign greets American POWs at Inchon during Operation Big Switch.

Some of these men had been in captivity since the first day of the war more than three years earlier.

swirling blades, and wave to the crowd. Those soldiers and other returning POWs got a hot shower, clean if ill-fitting fatigues, and some food before coming to us in the Counter Intelligence Corps for debriefing.

Our primary duty was to gather information about prisoners they knew weren't coming home, for whatever reason.

As we were explaining the procedure, several of the POWs struggled to hold up their heads. Some of these men had been in captivity since the first day of the war more than three years earlier.

A few had news about GIs reported as missing in action. Many of the MIAs had died of malnutrition, a disease such as malaria, dysentery or beriberi— or simply because they had lost the will to live. We filled out form after form. In quadruplicate.

On my last day, a colonel shuffled up to my table. Very thin and obviously ill, he sat motionless for several minutes before telling me he was an infantry division colonel and had been captured four days into the conflict.

He reached into a pocket for a mechanical pencil, holding it as if it were a precious jewel, and gently placed it on the table.

"Everything's right there," he said, instructing me to take the cap off and pull out the tube inside, but to do so carefully. "It damages easily."

Former POWs arrive in the U.S. at Pier 54 in San Francisco, California.

COMING HOME

The United Nations Command returned more than 1,000 Chinese and 5,000 Korean soldiers and about 450 civilians, while the communist side repatriated 684 UNC sick and wounded soldiers during Operation Little Switch, April 20 to May 3, 1953.

....

Operation Big Switch began Aug. 5, 1953, nine days after the armistice, and lasted until Dec. 23, 1953. It saw the repatriation of more than 87,000 POWs—about 12,000 UNC troops from the communists, and 75,000 Korean and Chinese soldiers from the UNC.

....

Some 20,000 captives, many of them Chinese Nationalists who supported exiled leader Chiang Kai-shek, refused to return to communist rule.

....

Prisoners on both sides who didn't want to go back to their home countries came under the care of a neutral nations commission for a short period. In time, many Chinese and Koreans were forced to repatriate anyway and faced persecution at home. A small number of former POWs were allowed to relocate elsewhere with help from the neutral commission.

I removed a 1-inch-wide cylinder of rice paper that was so tightly wound, it took some effort to loosen. Once it uncoiled, however, it stretched out more than 5 feet. On it were the names of 232 GIs who had died during the colonel's captivity, with rank, serial number and cause of death.

The thought of him carefully recording each name and protecting the list from the enemy for almost three years brought tears to my eyes. I stood and saluted him; I didn't know what else to do. Words would have been inadequate.

Hours later, the repatriates boarded the USS *General A.W. Brewster*, which was anchored offshore, for the final leg of their journey home.

Our reports from the debriefings were very vital to the War Department. The colonel and other captives had given the families of missing soldiers the gift of knowing what had happened to their loved ones and a chance to grieve their loss.

D. FRED BENTON
PORTLAND, OR

Back from the Abyss

Mother kept faith when faced with bad news.

M y grandmother declared: "No, my Isaac is not dead. He will come home."

She was steadfast after receiving a letter from the U.S. War Department telling her that her son was missing in action and had been officially declared dead.

My uncle Isaac Laughrun was raised on a small farm in Yancey County, North Carolina. He joined the Army Air Corps in 1940 and, in October 1941, was sent to Corregidor in the Philippines, promoted to sergeant, and made a machine gunner.

By 1942, the Japanese had cut off supply lines to the island. Gen. Jonathan M. Wainwright along with a few thousand men occupying the island were forced to surrender.

After a three-week stay in a converted prison in Manila, Isaac was sent to Manchuria. As a POW, he worked seven days a week, sunrise to sunset. The prisoners were paid one yen per day for their labor (in today's money, 113 yen equals $1) and often bought food from the peasants to supplement their poor diets.

They walked 8 miles from the camp to a factory and, because the camp was 18 miles from the Siberian border, it was often 20 to 25 degrees below zero. Isaac found a GI blanket and, with cords taken from cement bags, he fashioned a coat to wear over his Japanese-issued uniform.

"The camp was far from escape-proof," he said, "but where would you go?"

Three men escaped but were recaptured and shot as their fellow POWs were forced to watch. "The Japanese possessed a knack for making life unbearable," Isaac added.

The prisoners barracks were made of wood slats with a dirt floor. Heat came from a single potbellied stove and one scuttle of coal rationed every 24 hours. It was not uncommon to be talking to a man before you went to sleep and find him dead when you awoke.

When Isaac had time alone, he wrote in his diary. One entry reads: "I hope God will bless us and deliver us home; I pray every night that this war will be over soon."

Isaac embraces his mother, Martha Laughrun, before shipping out to the Pacific.

And one day it was. Russians liberated the surviving POWs at Mukden prison camp Aug. 20, 1945. Isaac arrived home weighing 96 pounds, down from 146. A few months later he married his childhood sweetheart, and they had a daughter, Brenda. After 54 years home, he died in 2000.

Isaac believed the suffering that he and his fellow soldiers endured was worthwhile—the price of freedom.

DAVID PETERSON
JOHNSON CITY, TN

Above, a day's rickshaw ride in what was Tsingtao, China, cost Leo and his buddies Moe and Schwartz a mere 25 cents. The three friends also bought the struggling family a meal. At right, Leo is all smiles after his discharge in 1946.

One Hitch Was Enough

His wartime stint in the Navy served him well.

M y father, Leo F. Gavlick, joined the Navy during World War II because all his friends were doing it. He was only 17 at the time and still in high school, so he had to wait for his assignment.

He chose the Navy because it meant he didn't have to sleep in the mud. But life on a ship was monotonous. Dad used to say, "They also serve who sit and wait"—and it well could have been the unofficial motto of his branch of the service.

In the war he served on the battle cruiser USS *Alaska* in the Pacific Theater. The *Alaska* took part in the battles of Okinawa and Iwo Jima, among others, where the ship saw action as a carrier escort. Dad witnessed firsthand the damage inflicted by kamikazes, the Japanese suicide pilots. He was a sight setter on the Quad 40, a 40 mm quadruple anti-aircraft gun, which might explain his postwar interest in pursuing education to become a civil engineer and surveyor.

Dad brought back a few souvenirs from the war, including a rifle (without the firing pin, of course) that he picked up from a pile confiscated from Japanese prisoners, and a Samurai sword he bought from a Marine who needed money for a poker game. He also got a strictly decorative Chinese sword from a street dancer.

It took many years before my father would talk about the war, but one highlight he liked to recount was dancing with Esther Williams, who he said was very tall. The future astronaut Wally Schirra was assigned to the ship for a short time. And Dad fondly recalled a stopover at Tsingtao (now Qingdao), China, where the Russian owners of a restaurant went out of their way to cook a Polish meal for him and his friends.

Though proud of his military service, Seaman Leo Gavlick knew, even at the tender age of 20, that one war was enough for one lifetime. He was honorably discharged in 1946.

BARBARA GAVLICK HARTNETT
SWOYERSVILLE, PA

WARTIME WORKERS

When companies recognized the efforts of those on the homefront.

1945 »

Men Are Back

When this Chrysler ad appeared in *Life* in January 1945, the tide of war that had started shifting with D-Day the previous June infused the Allies with hope for victory. That meant soldiers would soon be coming home. This image anticipates the transition: Female workers still in their factory coveralls look up at men dressed to take their place.

« 1942

A Varied Effort

This lively ad from Heinz, long identified with its slogan "57 Varieties," features pictures of real women doing essential wartime jobs, from munitions assembly and inspection to engine repair to communications and navigation. The last image, an illustration, represents the ideal that all those women are working for and that service members are fighting for: a peaceful family meal, with ketchup (naturally).

HARTFORD HANGOUT

My mother, Loretta Godwin, is on the far left in this photo taken in 1943 at a USO dance in Hartford, Connecticut. She was 18. I'm grateful for this picture because I have so few of her in her youth, and it reflects the camaraderie of sailors and gals getting a break from the war.

CARLA BOLLINGER · NEWBURY PARK, CA

GROWING UP AS ARMY BRATS

George and I were born six minutes apart on April 3, 1925. I was the older sibling, but George always called me "little sis." We even had our own language. George fought in both World War II and Korea, where his plane was shot down on June 13, 1952. I will miss him always.

JOANNE PATTON THOMAS
SAN DIEGO, CA

BANDS OF BROTHERS, YOUNG AND OLD

In Vietnam, I strove as a first lieutenant to make friends, share traditions and safeguard connections to home.

RONALD RALEIGH

MACON, GA

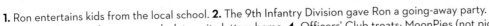

1. Ron entertains kids from the local school. **2.** The 9th Infantry Division gave Ron a going-away party.
3. Ron used a crate bottom as a desk to write letters home. **4.** Officers' Club treats: MoonPies (not pictured) and RC Cola.

AT THE WALL

The Vietnam Veterans Memorial, spearheaded by Vietnam veteran Jan C. Scruggs, was dedicated on Nov. 13, 1982.

Facts to know about the memorial:

The three-part memorial is one of the most-visited sites in Washington, D.C.

· · · · · · · · · · · · · · · · · ·

The Memorial Wall consists of 140 black granite slabs grit-blasted with the names of more than 58,000 fallen or missing military men and women who served in Vietnam.

· · · · · · · · · · · · · · · · · ·

The Three Servicemen and the *Vietnam Women's Memorial* statues are nearby.

· · · · · · · · · · · · · · · · · ·

No federal funds were used to build the memorial; donations came from more than 275,000 individuals and organizations.

· · · · · · · · · · · · · · · · · ·

Offerings left by visitors are collected and stored or become part of a traveling exhibit.

· · · · · · · · · · · · · · · · · ·

Visit *thewall-usa.com* to find a specific name.

Sp5c. James M. Sutton, March 1967

HOME WITH HONOR

WITHIN A YEAR OF GRADUATING IN 1965 from Father Judge High, an all-boys Catholic school in Philadelphia, Pennsylvania, most of us were drafted for the Vietnam War. When we returned, we didn't talk much about our service. But after 51 years away, I went back for the first time to see the old school. There in front was a monument for the 27 schoolmates killed in Vietnam. After seeing the names, I saluted them, sat down with my wife and cried.

Suddenly the door opened and schoolkids rushed to the monument to say a prayer. They do this every school day. It was such an honor to see these heroes, who paid the ultimate price for their school and this great country, remembered this way.

JAMES SUTTON • BRADENTON, FL

Dear Hank Wharton
    I hope you had a nice Chrissmtiss.
Gess whot Ching had kittons.
And one of the kittons. has its izz oppen

        To day Happy eat Jonhs food.
TOday is January 7/ / / 1967.
    you can see I I hed trubbl on the other
    Lien.
    AND I HAD TRUBBL ON THE DATE TO?
SPAHAY ON THE 7

                        LOVE
                        ROBYN WHARTON

(Especially)

ROBYN SENDS A LETTER

Above is the letter my son Henry Wharton
received from his 7-year-old sister Robyn
while he was stationed in Vietnam. He kept
it in his pocket until he returned home.
PAULINE WHARTON · NEW MARKET, AL

> *I was a cook for the Army
> in Cu Chi, South Vietnam.
> Two weeks before Thanksgiving
> we were running low, but fresh
> supplies arrived. I cooked
> like crazy and everyone
> ate really, really well.*
>
> **WELDON REESE**
> CHILDRESS, TX

WHAT ARE THE ODDS?

My brother-in-law Richard Morrison, 19, right, met his brother
Thomas, 20, during a 1967 night patrol in Vietnam. Both
survived and returned to their hometown of Canton, Ohio.
FRANCINE MORI · FLORAL PARK, NY

True Grit in Camp

On a third tour of Vietnam, star power emerged.

Freddie Richard Joseph Groen, Army specialist 5, headed back to Vietnam for his third tour in 1968, to produce a documentary for the U.S. Army.

Irish-born Freddie had grown up in Kings, Illinois, the oldest son of Mabel and Fred Groen. He enlisted in the Army in 1964 during the Vietnam War and was trained in audio technology and photojournalism.

By 1968, Freddie had been to Vietnam twice, for 16 weeks each time. As an audio specialist, he had the opportunity to interview top brass including Gen. William Westmoreland, plus various heads of state and other dignitaries.

He was embedded on a number of missions with the ground and air troops and filmed some dramatic and horrific battles. In one instance, he spent from daybreak to lunchtime inside a tank, filming war activity. He returned to camp, and his closest friend, Nils Peterson, took over to cover the action for the rest of the day. Less than an hour later, the tank was blown up by a land mine and Nils lost his life.

After this terrible loss and as the new father of a baby girl, Freddie hesitated to return to Vietnam for a third tour. He knew how fragile life was, especially in such a hostile environment. It wasn't until he landed in Vietnam the third time that he learned he would be filming a documentary with The Duke, John Wayne.

"Returning to Vietnam was worth it for the opportunity to spend time with The Duke," Freddie recalled.

John Wayne starred in the documentary Freddie filmed in Vietnam in 1968.

Working on the movie with a talented actor such as John Wayne was a distinct pleasure for Freddie. He brought home pictures and 8 mm films of the actor, noting what a positive force Wayne was and how friendly and compassionate he was with the troops.

Remembering that time with great fondness, Freddie told us that the actor never put on airs and had no problem showing everyone his nearly bald head. He ate with the soldiers, sat with them, answered their questions and praised them for their bravery.

Freddie died unexpectedly in a vehicle accident in 1973. We, his family, still cherish the pictures and stories he shared of his time in Vietnam.

CAROL GROEN MAUST
HOUSTON, TX

Home at Last

Finally, the yearlong wait was over.

For a year, I lived with our three daughters in Salina, Kansas, at Schilling Manor, a place affectionately called "the home for waiting wives." All 700 of us had husbands in Vietnam, Thailand, Greenland or Alaska, and we waited with our 2,500 kids for the men in our lives to come home safely from their military missions. My husband, Jim Down, was returning after spending the latter half of 1969 and the first half of 1970 in Vietnam.

As the date approached, our daughters Mara, 8, and Tania, 6, eagerly crossed days off our countdown calendar. But even as we discussed Daddy's return home, all was not well with Jennifer, 5. Her dad had been gone so long that her anger just continued to swell.

Mara, for her part, had begun acting out right after Jim left for Vietnam in May 1969. She thought it was my fault he left. Our pediatrician told her, "Your mom doesn't want your dad to be gone either." With those words, Mara turned 180 degrees and became a stalwart helper.

Tania just wanted everyone to be happy. She smiled, patted me and believed everything would be all right.

But Jennifer was certain her dad would never come home. Although Jim wrote letters and mailed audiotapes and gifts, she would say, "Daddy's gonna die there. He won't ever come home." She would not be comforted, asking pointed questions about the war, the people involved and people being hurt. It didn't help that a bombing range adjoined Schilling, a former air base.

Jim was expected home in early May, and in April I wrote to tell him that Jennifer was still really mad. "Don't expect her to come running to you when you get here," I advised.

Finally the day arrived when he would return—May 6, his 31st birthday. We went to the airport, a few minutes from our house, to greet him. Bursting with

Jim Down says goodbye to his three girls before boarding a plane for Vietnam.

excitement, I waited behind the fence with Mara, holding Mischief, our new hamster, and Tania. Jennifer stood at a distance, arms folded, solemn, watchful.

The moment Jim walked through the gate, the two older girls rushed to him, chattering and showing off the hamster. Jennifer just stood there unwavering until Jim went to her, gently placing his arm around her and kissing the top of her head.

Once home, Mara and Tania led Jim to the dining room to see his cake and gifts. Jennifer walked behind. When they reached the table, she walloped him 31 times as hard as she could. Those birthday spanks released all her pent-up anxiety, sorrow, mistrust and fear from the past year.

When she finished, Jim hugged her and she hugged him back. From that point on, Jennifer became his shadow and would not leave him alone. But best of all, he had been forgiven.

JAN DOWN · IOWA CITY, IA

Taking a break, Pete straddles a bomb before loading it onto the aircraft.

A Family Affair with Water

If it was good enough for his dad and uncles,
it was good enough for him.

The day after I turned 19, in 1965, I was working as a boating and canoeing instructor at Camp Fuller in Wakefield, Rhode Island. It was Friday, July 30, and my mother, Natalie, called to tell me that two Army recruiters had inquired about my whereabouts and were on their way to Wakefield, a 45-minute trip from my home in Pawtucket.

Considering my love of the water and the fact that my dad and all my uncles were Navy men, I scooted into the local recruiting office to join the Navy on the spot. They told me that their July quota was full, but that if I could wait until Monday they would sign me up. I had left word at camp where I was going, so I was expecting the Army guys to walk in the door at any minute.

After I explained my situation and my love of the ocean, the Navy offered me a three-month deferment. I signed it with a smile.

As I expected, the Army recruiters were waiting for me when I arrived back at camp, but I proudly displayed my signed deferment stating that I was now a U.S. Navy sailor. They smiled, shook my hand and wished me good luck.

Three months later I was at boot camp and then off to my duty station on the USS *Franklin D. Roosevelt*, CVA-42, homeported in Mayport, Florida. I was assigned to the flight deck, and after a few deployments during which we practiced landing techniques with pilots, the ship steamed to the Gulf of Tonkin in the South China Sea.

We worked hard running raids and support missions for our ground troops. But getting home was all we talked about. Today, I own a commercial fishing vessel out of Point Judith, Rhode Island.

PETER E. BRODEUR
WAKEFIELD, RI

FAMILY OF SERVICE

My sister Nancy Marion Herb served in the Navy WAVES from 1957 to 1961. At 18, she went to Bainbridge, Maryland, for basic training. After boot camp, she went to Chicago, Illinois, for training as a physical therapist. From there and for the remainder of her military career, she was stationed at the Bethesda Naval Hospital. Nancy and our two brothers followed in Dad's footsteps; he was in the Navy during World War II and at the Normandy landing on D-Day. I'm proud of them, but having my older sister serve was extra special.

CANDY MAE BURGERT

READING, PA

Candy's sister Nancy wears her uniform well. She enjoyed her nursing role.

Starched aprons were worn on rounds by DeLores and by Olive Jane Wipson of Madison, Wisconsin. Near left, DeLores poses in her service uniform.

CALLED TO SERVE

Arriving in Chicago, Illinois, from Rockford in 1944, I started Cadet Nurse Corps training at Michael Reese Hospital. I met many wonderful women who answered their country's call to serve during World War II, including classmates Mary Gorsche and Olive Jane Wipson. We wore gray dresses with starched caps, collars, cuffs and aprons—and our sleeves were never rolled up. All of us continued in the field of nursing.

DeLORES HOLLISTER COOK

WESTMINSTER, MA

SHE WASN'T A HORSE, SHE WAS A MARINE

THE ONLY ANIMAL TO HOLD official rank in the Armed Forces, Sgt. Reckless, a chestnut mare of just 13 hands (4½ feet to her shoulder), was a decorated combat veteran of the Korean War.

First Lt. Eric Pedersen of the Fifth Marines bought her for $250 at a Seoul racetrack in October 1952 to carry ammo and other supplies in hilly, rough terrain.

She saw combat after a month of intense training, which included learning to "hit the deck" (get down) while under attack and to stay calm amid concussive fire.

Her most valiant performance came in March 1953 during the crucial defense of Outpost Vegas.

The fight raging, Reckless hauled packs of ammo, each about 200 pounds, up a grueling 45-degree slope. On the way back, she carried wounded soldiers. She made 51 round trips, mostly on her own, in a field chaotic with flares and gun smoke.

She caught shrapnel above an eye and in a foreleg but kept going, earning two Purple Hearts.

"There had to be an angel riding that mare," Sgt. Harold Wadley, who served with her that day, told the Lexington, Kentucky, *Herald-Leader* in 2017. "She knew where her gun team was."

Robin Hutton, author of *Sgt. Reckless: America's War Horse* (2014), led efforts to honor the mare with three memorials. One is at California's Camp Pendleton, where Reckless died in 1968.

Top: Reckless carries an ammo pack down a hill in 1953. Bottom: A monument at Camp Pendleton, California, captures Sgt. Reckless in a Korean War battle. The National Museum of the Marine Corps in Virginia has a similar statue, and a third stands at Kentucky Horse Park.

Mike and his sentry dog, Duke, trained together for a tour in Vietnam.

Dog Day Empathy

Soldier forms a special bond with his canine partner.

D uke, my four-legged pal and member of the K-9 unit in Okinawa, Japan, was introduced to me in April 1970. He had been an Army sentry dog for five years and had five tours of Vietnam behind him. With that much service time, Duke was definitely well-seasoned.

During our first field training session, explosions were ignited all around us. My job was to hit the ground, and cover and protect Duke's eyes and ears with my left arm. My thinking was a bit slow that day. Maybe it was the Japanese beer from the night before, but when the explosions went off, I froze. Duke, on the other hand, lay down and waited for me to cover his head with my arm. My training slowly kicked in and when I looked down at him, he was staring at me with his big brown eyes as if to say, *Get your behind down and cover my face.*

When I finally made it to the ground and covered Duke's head, I lifted my arm to peek into his eyes.

They seemed to say, *Boy, I sure got myself a real winner this time. He's going to need some work.*

Given Duke's experience, the eight weeks of training went fast and easy.

Near the end of my service, I received a birthday card from my folks. It read, "We miss you! Happy 20th birthday! We hope to see you soon!" Tucked inside the card was a small note telling me that my grandmother had passed away that week. I was so sad after reading the note that I didn't feel like doing anything. But I had to go out on patrol that night with Duke.

While on patrol, Duke did something I had never seen him do before. He dropped his head and lowered his eyes, and I could tell that he was sensing my grief. Tears ran down my face, knowing that this canine pal of mine shared my pain.

MICHAEL COLBURN
GAYLORD, MI

In Tribute

Petty Officer 2nd Class Blake Soller and his military working dog
Rico stand at the Guam War Dog Memorial, which honors 25 canines
who died during the island liberation in 1944.

CHAPTER 7

MOTORING MEMORIES

The freedom to travel on the open road
with a new car or a motorcycle has
always been an exciting prospect.

Heavy Metal Thunder

Like lonesome cowboys on steel horses, bikers Wyatt (Peter Fonda)
and Billy (Dennis Hopper) search for meaning on the open road
in the 1969 movie *Easy Rider*, an icon of motorcycle culture.

Ernie Ward holds son David while daughter Ruthie sits on the hood during a trip to Colorado in 1959. The other Ward kids, Peggy and author Nancy, are in the background. Ernie had the wagon outfitted with a bug guard and a roof rack.

East or West, Their DeSoto Was Best

The perfect vehicle for big families who liked to roam.

Living in Missouri near the center of the country put my family in the position to travel conveniently either east or west, and every summer my dad, Ernie, loved to take us on road trips.

With its push-button transmission and rear-facing back seat, our 1959 DeSoto station wagon was deluxe travel in those days. It easily accommodated our big family—our parents, my three sisters, my brother and me. And Dad equipped the wagon with extras, such as a bug screen and a roof luggage rack.

He loved DeSotos. Our previous family car had been a 1953 DeSoto four-door sedan.

For our first vacation with the new wagon, we drove west into the Colorado mountains. The novelty of snow in the middle of summer prompted all of us to jump out of the car and make snowballs, which we launched directly at our father.

The next year had us heading east. On Cape Cod in Massachusetts, it took two cabins for all of us. We spent extra nights in Corbin, Kentucky, as we waited for repairs to the push-button transmission.

David, Nancy, Peggy, Mom (Marilee), Susan and Ruthie get ready for a picnic in the woods in 1960.

The Wards take a break while unpacking the DeSoto for a stay in a pair of cabins in Massachusetts.

I have fond memories of both of these trips.

It turned out that 1959 was the last year for the DeSoto station wagon, and only about 700 of them rolled off the assembly line that year. Sadly, Chrysler discontinued the last DeSotos with the 1961 model year.

At least ours lives on in the beautiful slides we took on Dad's Kodak Pony camera.

Our 1959 DeSoto station wagon was deluxe travel in those days.

NANCY WARD VAN GULICK
RAYMORE, MO

Three of the fab four, Dave, Jack, and Harvey, get ready to drive their latest heap, a 1940s-era Oldsmobile, to Nova Scotia in 1953.

Hunting Heaps for Sport

Car lovers on a quest for the Big One.

My big brother Harvey, our cousin Jack, friend Paul and I hunted heaps in the Rhode Island wilds in the 1950s. It was an open season that never seemed to end.

A heap is any rolling wreck that a farmer would gladly take $10 for to get the rust bucket out of his barn. We knew there were genuine antiques out there, waiting to be fixed up. So we hunted for them in Paul's blue '39 Willys—a heap in its own right (though we wouldn't say that to Paul).

One heap hunter we met had found a 1920s Cadillac behind a fish market, spent a year restoring it—and two more trying to get out the fish smell. (We saw that gem at a car meet, sniffed and agreed: two more years, at least.)

Our fascination with heaps began when we were living in New Jersey and Harv, then 15, spotted a rust-crusted 1931 Chevy sedan, with one of its doors in the back seat and its headliner hanging like Spanish moss. He named her Elouise.

Harv worked on the car through winter and spring, until one magical afternoon she coughed, shuddered and started! Harv took her for a triumphal spin down our driveway and back up to the garage door, where Elouise died, trapping the family Plymouth as our mother was about to pick up our father at the train station a mile away.

Dave's girlfriend, Pat, helps to clean a recent find. She wound up married to her heap hunter.

A heap is any rolling wreck that a farmer would gladly take $10 for to get the rust bucket out of his barn.

We were straining to get Elouise out of the way when across the lawn came Pop, tie and jacket over his arm, sweat darkening his shirt. Without a word, he flung open the garage door, started the Plymouth and used it to push Elouise almost to the street. Then he stomped inside to shower.

We moved to Rhode Island a short time later, Harv driving Elouise the whole way without so much as a backfire. We wept when Harv sold her, but there was bigger game to bag, including the '38 Studebaker we called Little Brown Jug and

the 1940s-ish Oldsmobile that took us on our rite-of-passage road trip to Nova Scotia.

And then there was the Big One—a 1929 Stutz Blackhawk touring car we found in an old shed. Imagine me dressed in a raccoon coat and boater hat, with a ukulele and the family bulldog, driving that Stutz in the Bristol, Rhode Island, Fourth of July parade.

What I'd give to own that holy heap today!

DAVID ROBINSON
LANESBOROUGH, MA

Taken by Storm

They had to keep a weather eye on their new purchase.

W hen my husband, Robert, and I saw a picture of a 1948 Plymouth recently, it brought back memories of buying our first car, which also was a 1948 Plymouth.

We were living in Portland, Oregon, at the time. New cars were at a premium then; you had to get your name on a list to buy one.

We'd saved enough in war bonds, so Robert had his name put on a waiting list for a Ford or a Chevrolet.

But by chance he was walking near a Plymouth showroom in downtown Portland and decided to go in and ask a salesman whether the dealership had a long waiting list for new car purchases. The salesman grinned. He pointed to a car on the showroom floor and told Robert he could buy that one right away.

It turned out that another couple had just turned down their option to buy it.

Robert didn't want the car to get away, so he agreed to buy it on the spot. But in the time it took for all the paperwork to go through, a storm dumped a foot of snow on Portland, and our new Plymouth ended up stranded in the showroom.

Every day for several days we would ride the streetcar into the city to admire our car through the dealership window, and smugly say to each other, "That's ours!"

DORIS MUIR
HAPPY VALLEY, OR

Doris and Robert took a picture of their '48 Plymouth once they were able to dig it out of the snowed-in dealership.

BY THE NUMBERS

The winter of 1948-'49 ranks 16th in snowfall for Portland, at 23 inches.

....

That winter also was the city's third coldest, with an average temperature of 35.3 degrees at the airport.

....

The next year, 1949-'50, Portland got 44.5 inches of snow, one of the snowiest on record.

....

Portland's average annual snowfall is around 5 inches.

1960 was the final year for this body style, which had debuted in 1957. The Ford F100 had options of a 292-cubic-inch V8 engine or a 223-cubic-inch six.

From Roadside to Road Warrior

Original factory parts revive a popular workhorse.

Back in 2008 in Willard, Utah, I found this 1960 Ford F100 truck for sale on the side of the road. It was primer gray and had many modifications, including a small-diameter replacement steering wheel, chrome American Racing wheels, and oversize sideview mirrors like the ones on a semitrailer truck.

I had previously owned a 1957 truck of the same make with optional wraparound rear window. I regretted selling it, so I jumped at the chance to own a truck with the same body style.

While this vehicle had decent rust-free bones and only 76,000 actual miles, it had a lot of rough spots. I tracked down the owner at a local bar, and we settled on a price of $1,000. I spent the next six years restoring it to factory condition, specifications and color with original replacement parts. I had to range far and wide for those parts, including

a tailgate and bumper I shipped in from North Carolina. The cab headliner is an original factory replacement, as are the radio antenna and cab floor mat.

I had worked every summer as a technician at a dealership garage while I was an assistant professor of industrial technology at Utah State University College of Engineering, so I had experience working on cars. I began my career as a high school automotive science teacher.

The Ford F100 has a classic design and was extremely popular in its day. More than 100,000 trucks were built in the 1960 model year. I've taken it to many automotive shows, including the Cache Valley Cruise-In held around the Fourth of July every year in Logan, Utah.

FRED DUERSCH JR.
LOGAN, UT

AUTO BEAUTY

Ads for cars may look different today, but the appeal of beauty and class still remain.

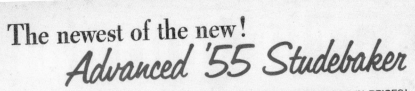

The newest of the new!
Advanced '55 Studebaker

NEW VISIBILITY! NEW COLOR! NEW POWER! NO INCREASE IN PRICES!

Windows you raise or lower automatically! These advanced new 1955 Studebakers offer the newest of the new in electrically controlled door windows—available for either the front-door windows only, or for all four sedan doors, as you prefer.

Newest surprise from alert, fast-moving Studebaker . . . a breath-taking additional line of 1955 Studebakers! Unexpected new visibility! Dramatic new two-toning! Tremendously increased power! All at no increase in Studebaker's low-level competitive prices! Marvelous power assists and air-conditioning, pictured here, are optional at extra cost. See your Studebaker dealer now. Studebaker . . . so much better made . . . worth more when you trade!

Newest of the new power brakes! A slight pivot of your foot from accelerator to brake pedal—and Studebaker's newest of the new power brakes stop your car swiftly, smoothly, surely. Optional in all models.

Newest of the new air-conditioning! Studebaker's advanced-design air-conditioning provides more cooling than 10 average home refrigerators —filters, dehumidifies and freshens the air. Optional in all Commander and President sedans.

Newest of new power seats! Just touch a finger-tip switch and the driver's seat moves forward or backward as desired. This convenience is optional in all Studebakers including Champions.

Newest of the new in ease of parking and steering! Studebaker power steering—advanced again for 1955—relieves you from tiresome and exasperating wheel tugging. Better still, its price has recently been reduced. Almost

See Studebaker-Packard's TV Reader's Digest . . . a new weekly feature on ABC television network

1955

Newest of the New
Options available in 1955 Studebakers put power at the driver's fingertips. Two-tone paint and wraparound windshields are classic era stylings.

Curbing Her Enthusiasm

Sometimes the journey to independence can take a quick turn.

I was eager to get my driver's license in the 1950s, but I had a full class load in high school and couldn't fit driver's ed into my schedule. So my father graciously offered to teach me in his '55 Chevrolet. He'd take me to a small street in our New Jersey town to practice signaling, turning, backing up and parallel parking.

Now, that Chevy was a no-frills version without fancy options like electronic directionals, power windows, power steering or automatic transmission. It took elbow grease to crank down the window to signal by hand, shift the engine into gear, and then turn the giant steering wheel to make the car go in the direction I wanted.

When the day came to try for my license, I aced the written exam—I'd studied the driver's manual in depth—and waited nervously for my road test.

The examiner was all business in his uniform and cocked hat, with a clipboard at the ready. I fired up the Chevy, and for the next several minutes executed all of the examiner's commands without hesitation. I was so proud of myself! All that practicing with Father had paid off—I had it down pat.

The test was almost over and we were nearing the motor vehicle office when the examiner said, "OK, make a right here."

As before, I immediately did as he asked and muscled that stiff wheel as hard as I could to the right. It was only when I jumped the curb and saw that I was headed straight for the building that I realized he'd meant for me to drive another couple of hundred feet to the lot entrance and *then* make the right!

If our '55 Chevy had been equipped with airbags like today's cars, I'm sure they would have deployed when we made that flying leap over the curb. It's nothing short of a miracle that neither of us was hurt and I hadn't damaged the car. But all I could think at the time was that I'd blown my chance to get my license.

Perhaps the biggest miracle that day was when the examiner signed the form showing I had passed the test.

You could say my rite of passage to the world of driving was a little bumpy. I have never forgotten it—and often wondered if the examiner ever forgot it either.

CAROL M. ELY · ROSELAND, VA

The 1955 Bel Air by Chevy is prized today for its smart design. Buyers could choose among a two-door wagon, a four-door sedan or a convertible.

HOW TO EXPAND YOUR HORIZON

OUR 1978 PLYMOUTH HORIZON WAS the sharpest little car on the road, with its gleaming white finish, shiny chrome accents and vinyl wood grain trim.

The Horizon was the first front-wheel-drive subcompact that Chrysler built in North America, along with its Dodge sibling, the Omni. It plowed through snow in the winter. In summer, the Horizon's air conditioning—a first for us—kept us cool, and the car seemed to go forever on a tank of gas.

We drove it to Florida for spring break, Cedar Point amusement park in Ohio in the summer, Pennsylvania in the fall, and family events throughout the year.

Our most memorable drive was in 1979 during a family picnic near Cleveland, Ohio. One of our cousins had moved to a new apartment and we all wanted to see the place, so we crammed everyone into the Horizon, taking back roads and ducking down whenever a police car drove past.

We felt like circus clowns, laughing like crazy, when we finally piled out.

MARK STEFFEN
WASHBURN, TN

Mark and passengers test the limits of the Horizon's seating capacity.

My younger sister Arline, 15, and I are fixing to go for a ride on my 1950 Powell scooter. We were only 15 months apart and attended California's Leuzinger High School, a rival of Hawthorne, where the Beach Boys went a few years after us.

ROGER VALENTINE · ROBERTSDALE, AL

A Stop at HoJo's Was a No-No

Dad smelled a conspiracy in the roadside restaurant.

How sad I was when I read that the last Howard Johnson's Restaurant, located in Lake George, New York, went up for sale. At one time Howard Johnson's was the biggest restaurant chain in the country, with more than 1,000 locations, almost all of them on major roads.

Even sadder for me is knowing that I never ate at or even entered a Howard Johnson's. It was as forbidden to me as cigarette smoking and underage drinking. My father, Paul, objected to the chain founded by Howard Deering Johnson for his own quirky reasons, which became clear during our summer family road trips to Myrtle Beach, South Carolina.

We'd load up our Buick LeSabre and take the Pennsylvania Turnpike out of Pittsburgh to Breezewood before heading south. On one trip, in 1968, the windows were open, fresh air was hitting us in the face, and the distinct outline of a HoJo's could be seen a short distance away. My sister Beth had a little problem.

"I have to go to the bathroom," she stated.

"You'll have to wait for the next exit," Dad said. He looked at our mother, who

Deborah hugs Beth (right), who launched an unsuccessful challenge of Dad's no-HoJo's law.

was reading the map. "How far to the next exit, Ev?"

"It looks like 25 miles."

"Twenty-five miles!" Beth groaned. "You've got to be kidding. There's a Howard Johnson's. Please, I have to go right now."

"Hold it," Dad told her.

"You want me to hold it so I'll have to use some creepy gas station bathroom where you have to get a key?"

"You will not patronize that highway robber," Dad shot back, referring to Howard Deering Johnson. "He has a monopoly on the turnpike."

Our father then went into this nutty cloak-and-dagger theory that the whole thing was fixed. "I wonder who he bought off to get such a sweet deal. It was a payoff for sure."

"I don't want to patronize the place," Beth argued. "I just simply want to go to the bathroom."

This conversation or a similar one was repeated a few times over the years, with the result that Beth and I understood capitalism, free trade, monopolies and other aspects of supply-and-demand economics—not to mention how to hold your bladder for long periods of time—before our peers.

But HoJo's was a mystery.

DEBORAH KOCH DIEHL
MONROEVILLE, PA

On the Trail of an American Dream

Couple travel the mother of all roads.

California-bound, Bob and Florence take a break during their epic journey to get dolled up and climb mountains in the Southwest.

Bob Snow and I married in 1945, shortly after we both were discharged from the military in Illinois. He had been an aircraft crew chief during the war and loved it, so he hoped to do the same kind of work in peacetime. His dream was to apply to the Flying Tigers, the country's first cargo freight airline, which was in California.

I was in love and would have gone to the moon with him, but California? That was beyond my imagination. It became very real in 1946 when we bought a Kozy Coach house trailer and outfitted it with birch cupboards, a sink, a water pump, a refrigerator and a space heater. Loaded, the little thing had to weigh 1½ tons.

"Now we can go to California!" Bob exclaimed. So we hitched the coach to our 1940 Plymouth coupe and headed west out of Chicago along Route 66.

Going through Missouri, we passed several handmade signs: See the Cave. These led us to an old farmhouse, where two elderly ladies welcomed us like old friends. They took turns explaining the natural formations in the cave and shooing away the bats, saying, "Don't scare the nice folks!"

The Oklahoma oil wells were an ugly part of the scenery for me, a farm girl raised in the green rolling hills of southwest Michigan.

Texas and New Mexico rolled by. In each little town we saw hotels, stores and gas stations in unusual styles, including tepees, pueblos and frontierlike storefronts. We'd stop nightly at a gas station, where for $5 or $10 we could plug into the electricity, fix our food, use the bathroom and bathe out of a basin. It was a simple, easy life.

In Flagstaff, Arizona, we left the trailer at a gas station to drive down a narrow, rocky road to the Grand Canyon, which was breathtaking beyond description. We happened to park near a couple from Galesburg, Michigan, and we all hugged as if we knew each other.

In the mountains, we passed several big cars on the side of the highway with radiators boiling over. Our coupe was performing beautifully, thanks to Bob, a top-notch mechanic who kept the car well-tuned. I was proud.

The mountain driving involved a lot of maneuvering around tight corners and up and down steep grades, but we finally reached the foothills, where we could see miles of flat road leading into Bakersfield, California. As we descended, we continued to gain speed, until I peeked at the dashboard and saw that we were going 82 mph.

I gripped Bob's arm. "I don't like to go this fast," I told him.

"I don't either," he said. "But we have no more brakes." We had to ride it out as best we could.

At the end of our journey we settled in at a Culver City trailer park. Bob worked for the Flying Tigers for several months until the company relocated to Burbank. We couldn't find a decent trailer park near there, so we moved on. We traveled as far as Oregon in hopes of finding another airline job for Bob before eventually deciding to head back home to Michigan.

After a terrifying haul east through the mountains on switchback roads beside 6,000-foot drops, I'd had enough of that Kozy Coach. We sold it in Reno, Nevada, to a couple who planned to take it to Alaska along the recently built Alcan Highway. I wished them good luck and blew a kiss goodbye to what had been our sweet little home for over a year. We'd seen a lot of the country together.

FLORENCE SNOW FINKEY
KALAMAZOO, MI

The Kozy Coach rolled along behind the Snows' trusty 1940 Plymouth as they made their way down Route 66. The trailer was the couple's home for more than a year.

THE ROOTS OF 66

America's first fully paved highway has a storied history.

Lt. Edward Beale, head of the U.S. Army Camel Corps, surveyed part of the route in 1857.

....

Established in 1926, it covers 2,448 miles.

....

Cyrus Avery of Tulsa, Oklahoma, oilman and loyal 66 booster, nicknamed it the Main Street of America.

....

An early 66 publicity stunt was the Bunion Derby, a 1928 footrace from California to New York. Cherokee runner Andy Hartley Payne won the $25,000 prize.

....

John Steinbeck called it "the mother road" in *The Grapes of Wrath*, his 1939 chronicle of Dust Bowl migrants.

....

It was decertified in 1985, but about 85 percent is still drivable.

Then, as today, the stretch of Route 66 through Arizona is one of otherworldly beauty.

SHE FELT THE KICKS ON ROUTE 66

LIFE WAS HARD IN ARKANSAS IN 1925. There was no work; people were going hungry.

So my parents, Henry and Ollie King, decided to hitch up a wagon and, with their three children, head out on Route 66 for California, the land of plenty. All was going well until they reached the desert. Ollie shook her head.

"Turn around," she said, "or we'll all die of thirst in that desert."

So they headed back toward Bonnerdale, Arkansas, but on the way, they ran into another small snag: It seems my mother was expecting a baby. I was born in the covered wagon on Route 66 near Sapulpa, Oklahoma.

I now live in Mountain View, very close to Arkansas State Highway 66.

HERSHEL KING
MOUNTAIN VIEW, AR

Driven to roam Route 66 in my brand-spanking-new Pontiac ragtop, a friend and I traveled from Ohio to California—and back again— in the summer of 1948.
LOIS ANN "TAN" GRAHAM
LIMA, OHIO

A TIMELY TRIP

SETTING OUT BRIGHT AND early that day in February 1964, I was eager to begin my trip west. I had just graduated from Purdue University and looked forward to driving a new blue Ford Fairlane 500—my graduation present—from my home in Rockville, Indiana, to California, where I'd accepted a job.

In St. Louis, Missouri, I lost sight of the other car I'd been traveling with while navigating the construction zone around the base of the Jefferson National Expansion Memorial— now known more famously as the Gateway Arch—which wouldn't be completed until the next year. I was relieved to be on my own; now I could drive without the constant worry of keeping another car in my rearview mirror.

On day three, I got to Flagstaff, Arizona, about 5 p.m., checked into a motel and settled in to wait out a snowstorm. The next morning there were at least 10 cars in the ditch within the first few miles I drove. I cruised on by, glad that those fierce Hoosier blizzards had taught me something about how and when to drive in bad weather.

I reached Pasadena, California, as the sun set, the valley before me an expanse of multicolored lights. Never before had I seen anything so exotic—it struck fear into the heart of this Indiana farm girl.

But it was a good kind of fear, for California was my land of promise: My solo flight along the Mother Road had brought me to the home of Douglas Aircraft, where the next week I would start my career as an engineer in the science and space division.

SHARLIE WOIWOD
ARVADA, CO

Reed Lesiak of Addison, Illinois, snapped this Model A Ford at a historic gas station in 2014 while on an antique auto club trip to Pontiac, Illinois, along The Old Road.

FINDING HIS WAY

At 20, I took a break from college to escape a brutal Wisconsin winter. Inspired by the TV series *Route 66*, about two guys experiencing the mystique of the road in a Corvette, I set out in January 1963 on what turned into a four-year odyssey.

My 1955 Chevy held heat for only about an hour, so I plowed through the northern section as quickly as I could. In New Mexico, I went through downtown Albuquerque in late evening. As night gave way to daybreak, the grandest sight of my Route 66 experience was before me: the mountains. That view of sun-drenched peaks is one I'll never forget. I saw beauty even in the desolate stretches as the expanse of Arizona desert carried me westward.

For me, Route 66 was more than an adventure. It was my passage to adulthood.

DICK LARDINOIS · CRIVITZ, WI

The Mendillos made a mad dash for New Jersey along Route 66 one Christmas.

Eastward Ho!

A holiday rush to the other coast.

—

Angel and I married in 1951, and shortly afterward I was drafted into the Army and assigned to the Presidio of San Francisco, California. We lived off post until I got my orders for Korea on Dec. 19, 1952. I had furlough until Jan. 3, so we decided to go home to New Jersey for the holidays.

We bought a used car and loaded it up. I had thought ahead and bought chains in case we encountered snow. That was the smartest thing I did, as we hit a storm at Tehachapi Pass in the Sierra Nevada mountains. Cars were sliding all around me, but I was able to stay on the road.

We had only a blanket to keep us warm. I wanted to drive straight through to make it in by Dec. 25, but we were so cold that in New Mexico I stopped to have a car heater installed. After that, the biggest danger was that I'd fall asleep at the wheel. We'd pull over for quick catnaps, and the rest of the time Angel recited nursery rhymes to keep me awake.

Meanwhile, the car burned oil. Whenever I topped it up I had to keep it running or it wouldn't start again until the motor cooled. I'd forget and have to flag someone for a push. We were lucky—people always helped.

We got home at 1:30 a.m. on Dec. 26—but it was 10:30 p.m. Christmas night, California time. So technically, we made it!

ALAN MENDILLO · WAYNE, NJ

RAISED ON THE ROAD

Route 66 is truly my Mother Road. I grew up in Fontana, then Azusa, and as an adult, I lived in Glendora—all on Route 66 in California. I married my husband, Ted, in 1960 at St. Frances of Rome Church on Route 66 in Azusa. It's still there and always packed on Sundays. Throughout the '60s and '70s, I worked at several businesses along Route 66, including a thrift store, a grocery, a boat dealer and the Foothill Drive-In Theatre in Azusa. They've all closed, although the Foothill's marquee is intact and the drive-in is sometimes used for special events.

I might add that I got my only traffic violation on Route 66. The officer who issued me the ticket turned out to be one of my neighbors.

KAREN MEYERS · TWENTYNINE PALMS, CA

When my car broke down near Roy's, I didn't have enough for the repairs, so I offered my wedding rings. I had to save up, but later I did return with the cash and got my rings back.

ANNE STANBROOK
SAN CLEMENTE, CA

Roy's Cafe and Motel in Amboy, California, is one of the most recognizable sights along old U.S. 66. Built in 1938 and expanded in the '50s, Roy's angled storefront and Googie-style sign have appeared in dozens of films and TV shows.

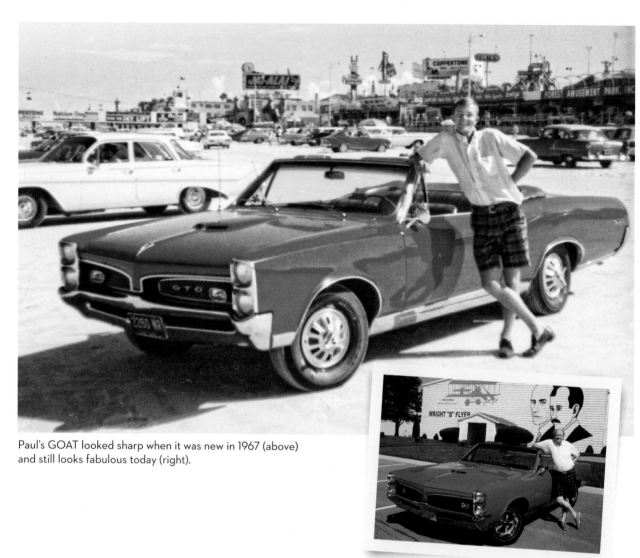

Paul's GOAT looked sharp when it was new in 1967 (above) and still looks fabulous today (right).

Ride of a Lifetime

He relives his carefree youth every time
he gets behind the wheel.

After graduating from Miami University in Oxford, Ohio, in 1967, I purchased this Pontiac GTO brand-new. I was 21 and bought it because it looked cool. I figured that if the girls didn't like me, they'd at least like my car.

It cost about $3,350 at a time when I earned $93 a week as an accountant. It came with a 400-cubic-inch, 255-horsepower engine; automatic transmission; power steering; bucket seats; and Firestone redline tires. I added the Rally II wheels later.

Back in the mid-1970s, when American automakers stopped production on most convertibles, I decided I had better hold on to this original muscle car. I have never raced or modified it—or had any

accidents with it. With 124,000 miles, my GTO is essentially a survivor with the original interior, chassis and factory-applied Regimental Red paint.

I drove it every day for 10 years to the high school where I taught business and marketing. I'm retired now after 35 years as a teacher, but occasionally I'll meet former students who ask me if I still have that red car.

The old GOAT (the car, not me) turned 50 last year and still looks remarkable. I tell people that the GTO is part of my youth. How many baby boomers still have the car they drove on dates back in their 20s?

PAUL MEYER · DAYTON, OH

Neon Aglow

Blue Swallow Motel, still family-owned, has been a Tucumcari,
New Mexico, fixture since the 1940s. Retro enthusiasts love its pink
stucco exterior, period furnishings and groovy neon sign.

CHAPTER 8

SEEING STARS

Remember the celebrities who influenced
the decades, and enjoy recollections
of starstruck encounters.

King of Swing

In a late 1930s movie appearance, Benny Goodman wails on his clarinet
while the orchestra follows his lead, rousing audiences
with a mix of Big Band jazz and swing.

A Day in Her Life

Starstruck fan puts her skills to work for her idol.

A fter seeing Doris Day in *Calamity Jane* when I was 10, I was hooked and determined to meet the lovely lady with the gorgeous smile and beautiful voice. I even started networking before it was a thing, eager to find other Doris Day fans.

Thanks to *Photoplay* magazine, I joined the only official Doris Day Fan Club, based in London, England. Through the club, I met other fans—Eileen, Hilda and Mary—who lived in the Los Angeles area. We became friends and kept in touch via letters and phone calls. My parents questioned why our phone bills were so high with calls to the West Coast. My plan was one day to travel there, meet my new friends and, with luck, see and meet Doris Day, too.

I made my first pilgrimage to Los Angeles on Aug. 15, 1965, by myself. Ironically, it was at the height of the Watts riots, and my parents were not thrilled that I had such a one-track mind. But I was determined to go.

Once in Los Angeles, I met my "Day Gang" buddies, but our efforts to meet Doris proved fruitless, despite driving past her Beverly Hills home countless times. Undeterred, I returned the following year. Again, no Doris.

By this time I'd graduated from Marian University in Indianapolis, majoring in English and journalism, and I'd landed a job as a reporter and feature writer for my home state *Indianapolis News*.

Persistent fans, my California friends eventually met Doris and told her I was making my third trip to Los Angeles and would love to meet her. Doris agreed, but no date or time was specified until finally, on Oct. 21, 1967, the day before I was to fly home to Indianapolis, my dream came true. Doris rode her bike to Bailey's Bakery, a local shop she frequented almost daily when she wasn't working, and met us for breakfast. I went into full reporter mode, asking about her next movie, her next record and more. Gracious, she answered every question, enjoying my enthusiasm.

I found Doris very down-to-earth, and we chatted like old friends. I told her that I wanted to move to the area; she encouraged the idea.

Much to my parents' chagrin, the following March I moved to Los Angeles, where my friend Mary and I lucked out by finding an apartment one block from Beverly Hills and within biking distance of Bailey's Bakery.

Mary and I looked forward to Saturdays when we would bike to the shop and have breakfast with Doris. We were thrilled when we saw her bicycle parked outside. Doris would visit with us, treating us like sisters and confiding about her TV show and her 11 dogs.

Soon after moving, I landed a job in public relations with The May Co. Then, on April 20, 1968, one month after I moved to the area, Doris' husband, Marty Melcher, died unexpectedly.

Bailey's Bakery, Doris and Mary Anne's frequent hangout, was a great place to discuss the issues of the day.

Doris' nickname for Mary Anne was Mairzy Doats, after a popular 1940s song Doris sang to her.

A few months later, the phone rang. It was Doris asking if Mary and I would meet her for breakfast at the farmers market and go shopping with her. We knew then that our friendship had gone beyond just being fans and a star.

A year later, I was in a car accident and broke both legs and my right arm. I was on disability for several months and, during my recovery, Doris and her mother, Alma, kept in touch with me.

While recuperating and before going back to work, I visited with Doris at Bailey's, our favorite hangout. At one point Doris said, "I'll bet you'd be a good secretary."

Two days after I went back to work, Doris called and asked me a single question: "How would you like to come work for me?"

I jumped at the chance, of course.

Every weekday I drove to her house, where her driver picked us up at 6:30 a.m. and took us to the CBS lot in Studio City to film *The Doris Day Show*. We always took three or four of her dogs with us. My duties varied. I was personal secretary, fan-mail response writer, dog walker, errand runner and assistant on many projects.

Then, two weeks before Christmas 1972, Doris' housekeeper abruptly left. Doris' mom had already made plans to spend the holidays with her family in Texas, so Doris would be alone. Knowing she would be overwhelmed, I volunteered to stay with Doris through the holidays. The housekeeper never returned, so those two weeks turned into almost two years.

My mother and friends back in Indianapolis were overjoyed that I got to live my dream.

Sounds like something that could happen only in the movies, right?

MARY ANNE BAROTHY · INDIANAPOLIS, IN

When he was 11 years old, Ron noticed that the Bradys lived in a cool house.

That's the Way He Became
The Brady Bunch

The '70s-era show left its mark.

From about 1970 to 1973, I must have watched every episode of *The Brady Bunch*, not because I loved the show, but because on Fridays it came on before *The Partridge Family*, which was my favorite. I waited excitedly through the chronicles of the Brady kids to see what David Cassidy and his rockin' family were up to each week.

Looking back, though, I've come to recognize that aside from their music, the Partridges had little influence on me, while the Bradys have shaped me in all sorts of ways.

I yearned for the Bradys' California sun, fancying myself a landlocked beach boy separated from his spiritual home. The large lots, green lawns and wide streets where the Bradys lived cemented in my mind the picture of the perfect neighborhood.

I was equally taken with the look of the Brady house—big backyard, flat driveway, carport with basketball hoop, and the open space inside, with floating staircase, exposed brick walls and artwork. Years later, I adopted a similar decor in my home, one free of clutter and with plenty of art for color. I even wound up with a Brady-style car, a 1970 Plymouth Barracuda.

Just as influential were the storylines. Some reflected my life—Peter overcoming his fear of the school bully, Buddy Hinton, for instance, or Greg resisting the pressure from his bandmates to smoke cigarettes.

Some episodes involved writing, which became my profession. It must have left an impression on me when Carol Brady wrote an article about her family for *Tomorrow's Woman* magazine. Like Carol, I saw value in the seemingly mundane and wrote about it, often seeing my work published. In another episode, Marcia composed an essay for a newspaper's Father of the Year contest. Following her lead, I wrote tributes to both of my parents that also made it into print.

Critics have bashed the show for being facile, but the truth is *The Brady Bunch* was ahead of its time in many ways, especially in its celebration of the blended family.

Watching the show now is like paging through a photo album. Familiar images bring back thoughts and feelings I'd long forgotten, and remind me where my ideas and aspirations originated. It's no wonder that I continue to enjoy *The Brady Bunch*. And I'm happy to be under its influence still.

RON BAXENDALE II
BROOMFIELD, CO

The Brady Bunch kids in 1969: Susan Olsen (Cindy), Maureen McCormick (Marcia), Christopher Knight (Peter), Barry Williams (Greg), Eve Plumb (Jan) and Mike Lookinland (Bobby).

Driving west, their shiny black car transported the family—from left, Maude, Walter, Patricia and Margaret—to California.

Can Curly Top Come Out to Play?

When in California, find out where the stars live.

The Dust Bowl and the Great Depression were two good reasons to leave Ardmore, Oklahoma, in June 1934. I was only 4 but I remember being tucked into bed with the covers pulled over my head and told to stay put while my mother, Maude, lined the windowsills with wet towels. Many who lost their jobs headed to California.

My dad, Walter, a newspaperman, had no trouble finding a job wherever we lived. A friend of his had gone to Alameda, California, and wrote back saying there was an opening for a pressman on the *Alameda Times-Star.*

My mother and my sister Margaret, 16, were thrilled about the move. California was where the movie stars lived, and Mother especially loved Shirley Temple and Mary Pickford.

Daddy bought a new used car. Mother packed and we waved goodbye to the neighbors. Daddy drove with my black kitten clinging to his shoulder. Mother sat in the front giving directions. My sister and I sat in the back singing "California, Here I Come" and "On the Good Ship Lollipop" all the way there.

When we reached Southern California, Daddy was tired and wanted to find a place to sleep. But Mother had a different idea. She bought a map from a gas station to find out where Shirley Temple lived, and soon we were parked in front of the star's home. To our surprise, it was just an ordinary-looking house in an ordinary neighborhood.

Mother told me to knock on the front door and ask if Shirley could come out and play. I did as I was told and a tall young man opened the door. He called out, "Mom, a little girl wants to play with Shirley!"

And what do you know? Down the stairs came Shirley Temple, her blond curls bouncing. She came right outside to where I was standing with her brother.

Then Mrs. Temple came out to say hello. At that point my mother and sister got out of the car and started talking with Mrs. Temple, while Shirley and I stared at each other as little kids do. Daddy stayed in the car with my kitten, wishing he could get back on the road and find a place to sleep.

PATRICIA GRIPON WALDRON
REDDING, CA

FUN FACTS

Shirley Temple went from child star to diplomat as a U.S. ambassador to Ghana and Czechoslovakia.

Born: April 23, 1928

．．．．．．．．．．．

Died: Feb. 10, 2014

．．．．．．．．．．．

Children: Three; a son and two daughters

．．．．．．．．．．．

Films include:
Little Miss Marker 1934
Now I'll Tell 1934
Bright Eyes 1934
Curly Top 1935
Poor Little Rich Girl 1936
Wee Willie Winkie 1937
Heidi 1937

Face-to-Face with a Gunslinger

A love of TV Westerns came in handy.

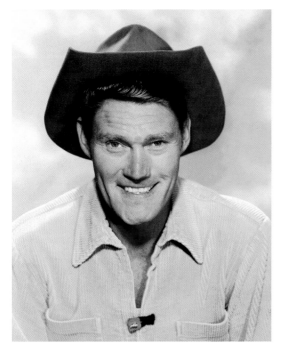

Chuck Connors starred as widower Lucas McCain in *The Rifleman* from 1958 to 1963.

My mother, a dyed-in-the-wool Democrat, was serving along with three other women as an election judge in one of Chicago's municipal elections on April 3, 1979.

During a lull in voter traffic, common during the hours when most people were at work or school, one of the polling officials came in with a huge smile on his face.

"I have a surprise for you," he said. "Be back in a minute."

He went to the doorway, beckoned with his hand and stepped aside.

In walked a tall, handsome man. The women were speechless. My mother was the only one among them who instantly knew who the man was. "You're the Rifleman!" she blurted out with immediate recognition.

The man grinned and in his deep Brooklyn accent replied, "That's me. Chuck Connors, in the flesh."

Sure enough, standing there was the former Chicago Cubs baseball player turned Hollywood actor.

Everyone was thrilled, but no one more so than my mother. Westerns were her thing. She loved John Wayne and all of his ilk. During the golden age of television, when Western dramas were on nearly every channel, she devoured them. She taught us to enjoy them as well.

As it turned out, Mr. Connors was in town visiting a friend who lived in Chicago. The actor sat and talked with my mother and her colleagues, but because the others were so dumbfounded, my mother carried the entire conversation.

She later said Mr. Connors was as nice in person as he was on screen. Then she pulled a folded sheet of paper from her purse and showed us his autograph. A huge C enveloped the remaining letters of Chuck and Connors on the page.

We were entranced. I still keep the paper bearing his signature, dated April 3, 1979, in my Chicago Cubs scrapbook.

MARTHA F. GRIEASHAMER
CHICAGO, IL

CLOSE-UP: CHUCK CONNORS

Born Kevin Joseph Aloysius Connors on April 10, 1921, in Brooklyn, New York.

....

Played two professional sports: basketball with the Boston Celtics during the 1946-'47 season and baseball with both the Brooklyn Dodgers and the Chicago Cubs.

....

Received $500 for his first acting role, a police captain in the movie *Pat and Mike* (1952), starring Spencer Tracy and Katharine Hepburn.

....

Left professional sports in 1953 to act full time.

....

Inducted into the National Cowboy Hall of Fame, 1991.

....

Appeared on the cover of *TV Guide* six times.

....

Died on Nov. 10, 1992.

John Martin stands to baseball legend Babe Ruth's left. His family treasures this photo.

Big on the Babe

Hanging with a Yankee slugger was a wartime plus.

G rowing up during the Depression in the 1930s, my father, John Martin, played baseball at Automotive High School in Brooklyn, New York. He was good enough to be recruited to play on the New York National Guard team in 1938. The country was still struggling and times were tough, so he enlisted with the 212th Coast Artillery and traveled around the Northeast playing baseball while getting paid for it.

At a game on Long Island, he met a high school girl named Dorothy from the small town of Baldwin. They started dating and writing letters.

In 1941, my dad re-enlisted in the Army with the 355th Anti-Aircraft Artillery Battalion and was sent to California to help guard the coastline. His unit was stationed at Santa Monica Beach, where local movie stars and national celebrities often visited. He collected a handful of autographs and photos of the stars and sent them back to Dorothy in New York.

But Dad's most treasured encounter with a celebrity came when the great Yankee powerhouse Babe Ruth paid a visit to the area and to my dad's battalion.

The Babe signed autographs and posed for photographs with the soldiers. My father got to talk baseball with perhaps the greatest hitter of all time.

Soon after Babe's visit, Dad's unit was sent to North Africa, where they fought in the Tunisia campaign. They went on to Italy and fought in the North Apennines and Rome-Arno campaigns. When the war was over, he returned home and married Dorothy. They were together for 64 years.

BILL MARTIN
MEDFORD, OR

CLOSE-UP: BABE RUTH

One of five inaugural members inducted into the National Baseball Hall of Fame in 1936.

....

Other 1936 inductees: Ty Cobb, Honus Wagner, Christy Mathewson and Walter Johnson.

....

Set both pitching and batting records.

....

Nicknames included The Sultan of Swat, The Bambino and The Colossus of Clout.

....

Holds record for most home runs in a decade: 467 in the 1920s.

It's Who You Know

Touching base with best contacts pays off.

———

My dad, Alton R. Kaste, was a general news photographer for the *Chicago Tribune* for 30 years. During that time, he had contacts with many fellow photographers from area newspapers, including the *Sun-Times* and *Daily News*, and with United Press International photo staffers and others—especially those who covered Chicago sports teams.

On a number of occasions, once at Wrigley Field (home of the National League Chicago Cubs) and again at the old Comiskey Park (home of the American League Chicago White Sox), my twin brother, Brad, and I were photographed with several of the pro ballplayers.

On a Thursday afternoon in the summer of 1956, most likely July 26, the White Sox were playing the dreaded New York Yankees at Comiskey Park. One of Dad's photographer buddies cajoled star player Mickey Mantle into stopping for a quick photo with Brad and me before the game.

If memory serves me correctly—we were only 10 then—Mickey was somewhat hesitant when asked to pose with us but finally gave in. No telling why he was looking off to his right when the photographer snapped the shutter, but that's clearly a wad of chewing tobacco in his left cheek.

I don't remember the final score, but the Yankees probably won, as they regularly feasted on the lesser pro ball teams of that era.

HOWARD F. KASTE
MORTON GROVE, IL

Real-life double header twins Howard, left, and Brad met baseball legend Mickey Mantle at Comiskey Park.

Celebrity Spec Replacement

It was an opportune time to be in the optical field.

John gave Mel Torme, right, a peek into his eyeglass business.

My wife, Joan, and I were big Mel Torme fans, so when he opened in May 1965 at The Royal Arms nightclub in Buffalo, New York, the two of us, along with another couple, attended the performance. I took a chance and half-jokingly sent my business card to his dressing room, by way of our waiter, with a note requesting a visit with the performer.

For the next hour we fully enjoyed the entertainment as part of the enthusiastic crowd. We were about to leave when the waiter informed me that Mr. Torme wished to see Mr. Zilliox. Joan looked at me and noted, "He said Mr. Zilliox, not Mr. Zilliox's party. We'll wait for you here."

So I got up and accompanied the server to Mel's dressing room. He was changing into a casual robe, and I was surprised by his greeting. "What luck," he said. "After landing my plane at the airport, I can't find my flying glasses. I must have lost them, and who walks in my dressing room but an optician."

After some introductory small talk, I stumbled into the only question I could think of—did he like being called the Velvet Fog? He didn't, and the conversation turned back to his concern about his lost glasses.

What he wanted were not prescription glasses, but a type of Ray-Ban sunglasses with the bottom half of the lens clear for reading the instrument panel inside the dark cockpit. And yes, I had a pair of these special sunglasses in stock at my office in South Buffalo.

"I'll be there tomorrow morning," he said. "How do I get there? I can borrow a car from my manager."

About 2 p.m. the next day, Mel arrived and I was ready with a photographer. I thought it best to ask permission, so I said, "Do you mind, Mel?" With a smile he said, "Not a bit."

After I fitted him with the pilot glasses, he stayed around for a while and chatted with the other people in the office. We had a wonderful visit.

Ever since that day more than 50 years ago, listening to Mel Torme's records has taken on a personal touch for Joan and me. We still talk about the day the star came to our office.

JOHN ZILLIOX · WILLIAMSBURG, VA

CLOSE-UP: MEL TORME

Melvin Howard Torme, the man with the velvet voice, sang pop, jazz and scat with classic style and ease.

....

Born on Sept. 13, 1925, in Chicago, Illinois.

....

Died on June 5, 1999, in Los Angeles, California.

....

Entered show business at 4, singing with the Coon-Sanders Orchestra.

....

At 8, starred on radio.

....

At 17, played drums in Chico Marx's band.

....

Won Grammy Awards for best jazz vocalist (male) in 1982 and 1983.

....

Also an accomplished songwriter, pianist, actor and author.

Always dapper actor Larry Hagman wore a signature Stetson cowboy hat as J.R. Ewing in the TV series *Dallas*.

Saved by the Bell

Those chicken scratches were indecipherable.

Thirty miles west of Fort Worth, Texas, is a charming little place and my hometown, Weatherford. The town was also home to Broadway legend Mary Martin and her son, Larry Hagman. I went to high school with Larry, and in 1949 we worked together on the school newspaper, *The Grass Burr*.

One day Larry walked into the typing room and handed me a piece of paper on which he had written something. He said, "Wanda, would you type this up for me?" I said sure, took the piece of paper, looked it over and thought, *Oh my gosh! I can't read a word he wrote down.*

Just then the bell rang. I handed the paper back and told him I had to get to my next class.

Larry graduated at the end of that school year. I graduated the following year, but after our time on the paper, I never saw him again.

When Larry was on *I Dream of Jeannie*, I couldn't believe how he looked. When we were in high school, he was a tall, skinny kid with ugly horn-rimmed glasses.

Once, while Larry was on the hit television series *Dallas*, my husband and I were checking in at an airport in Ireland to fly to London, then on to Dallas. The young woman who checked us in said, "I've been wanting to ask someone from Texas if the characters on the TV show *Dallas* are really from Texas."

"I don't know about the rest of the actors," I told her, "but I know Larry Hagman is from Texas because I went to high school with him."

She beamed with delight. She said her dad loved that show; she could hardly wait to tell him that she had met someone who actually went to school with J.R.

As it happens, my husband and I were probably the only people in Texas who didn't watch *Dallas*.

WANDA BAKER
BURLESON, TX

CLOSE-UP: LARRY HAGMAN

Born on Sept. 21, 1931, in Fort Worth, Texas.

....

Best-remembered TV roles: Major Anthony Nelson, *I Dream of Jeannie* (1965-'70); J.R. Ewing, *Dallas* (1978-'91)

....

On his new image after *I Dream of Jeannie*: "I was in *Jeannie* for some time and I made the transition to a bad guy from a rather bumbling idiot. ... I'm going to have a lot of fun with this."

....

On his role in *Dallas*: "People I meet really want me to be J.R., so it's hard to disappoint them."

Watch Out!

That newfangled way of seeing movies took him by surprise.

B y the time I turned 10 in 1952, I was an inveterate movie buff. Saturdays would find me at one of the three local theaters in town, where for a quarter I could see a double-feature, usually Westerns, with money left over for a Coke and a bag of popcorn.

In those days no one worried about being there at the start of the film. You paid your admission, picked up whatever refreshments you wanted and walked into the theater. If the movie was already in progress, you'd sit through the rest of it and the next one, plus all the shorts, cartoons and coming

attractions, until the first feature started again and reached the point where you'd come in. Then you left.

One Saturday, I decided to pass on my usual cowboy fare because there was a new kind of movie in town. *Bwana Devil* had been made in something called 3D, which I'd heard my classmates talking about. They said the 3D effect made it seem as if you were part of the action, but since none of them had actually seen a 3D movie, I couldn't be sure they were right. All I really knew about 3D was that you had to wear special glasses to see it.

The world's **FIRST FEATURE LENGTH** motion picture in **3 DIMENSION NATURAL VISION**

A LION in your lap!

A LOVER in your arms!

BWANA DEVIL

in THRILLING COLOR

starring ROBERT STACK · BARBARA BRITTON · NIGEL BRUCE

Moviegoers enjoy the 3D action of *Bwana Devil*. Critics panned it, but the movie made $95,000 in its first week and went on to make a fortune for United Artists. *Bwana Devil*, about man-eating lions in Africa, started the 3D craze in 1952. The novelty gave 1950s movies an edge over TV for a short time before fading.

I paid my dime at the box office and was handed a pair of glasses that seemed to be made of construction paper, with gray lenses and a notch for my nose. I put them on and stopped at the concession counter for my usual Coke and bag of popcorn. I could hear that the movie had already started, so I pushed aside the curtain and entered the theater.

I looked up at the screen just in time to see someone throwing a spear at me! Now, I may not have known much about 3D, but I did know that when someone throws something at you, you try to avoid it. I hit the deck, my drink and popcorn flying everywhere, then I looked around to see if the spear had stabbed someone behind me. I peeked at the movie again, and this time I realized that everything I'd heard about 3D was true—things really do appear to jump off the screen.

Back I went to the concession counter for more popcorn and another Coke. The woman who served me noticed that I was wearing most of my previous drink and said something about how realistic 3D was. I had to agree with her.

KEN WOOD
ROUND ROCK, TX

Carleen kneels next to Susan shortly before they left for Reno, where they caught Liberace fever.

A Ringing Endorsement for Mr. Showmanship

Reluctant concertgoers emerge fans of Liberace.

My co-worker Susan's parents offered to take her to Reno, Nevada, in 1963 for her 21st birthday, and she invited me to go along. When we arrived, they left Susan and me alone to do whatever we wanted. We both longed to see a live show, but to our dismay the only one we could get tickets for was Liberace's.

When I was growing up, my parents always watched *The Liberace Show*. I got so sick and tired of hearing him say "thank you, thank you, thank you, ladies and gentlemen" that I preferred doing my homework to watching him.

Susan didn't want to see him either, but we were determined to see a stage performance, and Liberace was our only choice. We were still trying to pronounce the name listed with him on the marquee, "Streisand," when we took our seats.

Well! All I can say is that Liberace put on the best show I have ever seen, and I've seen a few

since then. At one point, he did the twist across the stage and then said, "What I don't like about the twist is I always have to pull down my shorts afterwards." And he turned as if to do just that, though he yanked only at the material of his trousers. I think I clapped the loudest of anyone in the audience. Barbra Streisand walked onstage carrying a wooden barstool. She wore a sailor-style white blouse with red trim and a blue skirt that reached the floor. One of my favorite tunes she sang that evening was "Who's Afraid of the Big Bad Wolf," which was a hit for her at the time.

Barbra has been my favorite female singer since that day. We were both 21 then, born the same year, 1942.

The memory of those exciting performances is still etched in my book of life.

CARLEEN BUBENIK
SANGER, CA

Sandra posed with Merle in Chicago, Illinois, in 1967 (left), and again in Countryside, Illinois, in 1982 (below), as her brother-in-law Bobby slipped into the picture—a move her son Harry calls "photo-bombing before it was photo-bombing."

Ramblin' Fever

She followed Merle Haggard in concert for decades.

There were no jobs to be had where I grew up in Boone County, West Virginia, in the 1960s, so I moved to Chicago, Illinois, to look for work.

There I met a friend from Tennessee, who talked me into going with her to a country music club to see an up-and-coming singer named Merle Haggard.

After the show, we went backstage to meet him and have our picture taken with him.

From that day on, I was hooked on his music. I bought his records and played them for my future husband, Harry Blomstrand, who was a Chicago police officer. Harry in turn played them for his brother Bobby. It wasn't too long before the whole family was hooked on The Hag.

After Harry and I got married, and as our family was growing, we tried to attend every one of Merle's concerts within driving distance of Chicago.

At a show in Countryside, Illinois, in 1982, I happened to bring along the pictures of Merle and me that were taken in 1967. I showed them to Merle's piano player, who took them to the singer. We could see Merle laughing as he looked

at them. After a few minutes, he came off the bus to talk to me.

"Boy, we sure have changed a lot since then," he said.

"Yes," I joked. "We got a lot better looking."

"Well, I don't know about that," he said, laughing. "But let's update these pictures."

So he posed with me again while my husband snapped the picture. I didn't know until I had developed the film that my brother-in-law Bobby had sidled into the background.

After that, we'd wait outside Merle's bus at the end of every concert. He'd always come out to talk with us and was very gracious. He got to know us pretty well as big fans and would invite us onto his tour bus.

At the last Merle Haggard concert we attended in Illinois, we had a party of 19 family members and friends with us.

On April 6, 2016, my son Harry called me. "Mom, Merle Haggard died today."

Merle died on his 79th birthday. I still miss him.

SANDRA BLOMSTRAND · ROCK FALLS, IL

Sunny day, sweepin' the clouds away on the set of the PBS series *Sesame Street*, Big Bird towers over the adults and kids. Other Muppets, from left, include Betty Lou, Bert, Grover, Roosevelt Franklin, Ernie, Cookie Monster, Oscar the Grouch and Count von Count.

When John Travolta and Karen Lynn Gorney hustled their way into our hearts in *Saturday Night Fever* in 1977, they ushered in a glittering age of Bee Gees hits, mirror balls and giant lapels.

The U.S. hockey team upsets the Soviets 4-3 in the medal round of the 1980 Olympics, in Lake Placid, New York, before a partisan crowd. With less than 10 seconds left, announcer Al Michaels asks, "Do you believe in miracles?," dubbing the game the Miracle on Ice.

In a heavily hyped tennis match known as the Battle of the Sexes, has-been Bobby Riggs, 55, challenged Wimbledon champ Billie Jean King, 29, to an on-court duel on Sept. 20, 1973. The game remains the highest-attended tennis match in U.S. history, and some 90 million TV viewers also watched King win.

RIGHT: DISNEY/KOBAL/REX/SHUTTERSTOCK

Bunny hugs Elvis Presley on one of her bike visits to his house.

Cola with the King

Before stardom hit, he was just a guy three blocks away.

———

My husband and I were married in August 1954. We spent short stints in Alabama and Utah before moving to Memphis, Tennessee, in the spring of 1955. The Elvis Presley phenomenon was in its early stages then; "Hound Dog" and "Don't Be Cruel" wouldn't come out until July of the following year, which was only a few weeks after the birth of our first child, Nora.

We were so far from family and friends, my mom suggested sending my sister, Beverly, 13, to stay with us to help with the baby, which ended up being a good idea for everyone. Beverly, or Bunny, as we called her, loved horses, and one of the colonels on base who kept a horse let my sister ride it often that summer.

While Bunny was staying with us, we learned that Elvis and his parents lived only three blocks from our apartment. So when she was done horseback riding and helping me with the baby, Bunny would ride her bike over to Elvis' house. As it turned out, Gladys Presley was a true southern lady. She always invited my sister in for a soda.

I regret never joining Bunny on her bike rides; within a year, Elvis bought Graceland and moved with his family out of the neighborhood.

LORRAINE O'BRIEN · PARAMUS, NJ

As it turned out, Gladys Presley was a true southern lady.

M-I-C-K-E-Y

Memorable Mouseketeer Annette Funicello sang and danced
her way to stardom on Walt Disney's *The Mickey Mouse Club* from
1955 to 1958. Her later feature films include *The Shaggy Dog*
and early '60s beach party romps with Frankie Avalon.

CHAPTER 9

HOLIDAYS AND CELEBRATIONS

No matter what time of year it is,
family and tradition make special occasions
all the more special.

Christmas in Pajamas

On a hectic Christmas in the early 1960s, I took a moment
to check out a toy with my sons Daryn and Lee Jr.

LEE TURNER · NORWOOD, NEW YORK

Crowds packed the Independence Mall area of Philadelphia, Pennsylvania—including the Liberty Bell Pavilion, foreground—for the bicentennial parade on July 4, 1976.

Everyone Loves a Parade

Drumbeats echoed as freedom rang.

D espite seeing only the tops of tubas, flagpoles, tricorn hats and President Gerald Ford's head, I have the best red, white and blue memories of being in the very place where the first Fourth of July happened 200 years earlier.

As a native Philadelphian and a newly minted member of Friends of Independence National Historical Park, the first chartered Friends group in the National Park Service, I was eager to staff the table across the street from Independence Square, where I promoted Friends membership and activities. However, at 5 feet 1 inch, I had a hard time seeing over the taller members of the crowd.

But what a sight to see and feel. President Ford's speech was deliberate but moving. The music stirred and flags inspired as the five-hour parade streamed by and floats from every state captured our imaginations. Most of all, the feeling of pride in our country was palpable.

It was an honor to be there and feel the patriotism that our country's founders, both men and women, had inspired in 1776.

LINDA ABBY FEIN • PHILADELPHIA, PA

DECORATED CYCLISTS

In Fort Collins, Colorado, riding bikes in the Fourth of July parade is a blast. Riders get involved by decorating their rides with streamers, flags and crepe paper.

RANK AND FILE

The U.S. celebrated its bicentennial throughout the year in 1976. On July 4, millions lined the streets of downtown Philadelphia as a parade including Colonial soldier re-enactors marched past Independence Hall, where 200 years earlier the Declaration of Independence was signed.

RED, WHITE AND BLUE

STEPS IN TIME
Majorettes march in a Fourth of July Freedom Festival Parade—a tradition in Linton, Indiana—in the 1950s.
LINTON VISITORS BUREAU · LINTON, IN

WINNING THE TRIFECTA
Thanks to Mom's sewing, my sisters and I stole the show at the 1954 July Fourth parade in Hammond, Wisconsin. From left, Mary took first place dressed as a queen, Shirley took second place playing Uncle Sam, and I took third as a farmer gone fishing.
KAY GEURKINK
BALDWIN, WI

OLD GLORY
I took this shot on July 4, 1959, when a neighbor suggested staging an Iwo Jima-inspired flag raising. From left are Bill Evans; John Price; my husband, Charles; and John's sister Martha.
BARBARA HOWELL
COLLINGSWOOD, NJ

My husband, Eldon, was 3 on July 4, 1941,
shortly before America joined the war.
Patriotism was strong at the time.

E.M. "COOKIE" MILLER
YELM, WA

Not at All the Great Pumpkin, Charlie Brown

This Halloween stinks!

My twin sister, Tracey, and I were 4 and our sister Margaret was 6 when we posed for a photograph (below) on Halloween 1967. Our sister was dressed as Casper the Friendly Ghost while Tracey and I wore the hobo masks that I am sure my mother bought at the dime store. With six children, my parents didn't have a lot of money for costumes. Every Halloween my mother got out those masks, and Tracey and I had to wear them if we wanted to go out trick-or-treating. Every year.

And every year we collected our Halloween candy in big paper bags from the grocery store. The one notable exception occurred in 1975. We were 12 and, yes, still using those hobo masks, but that year my mother had bought a plastic jack-o'-lantern to hold the candy she would pass out to trick-or-treaters. I begged her to let me use it instead so I wouldn't have to collect my treats in a paper bag. I whined and fussed profusely until I finally got my way.

I was so proud to carry that jack-o'-lantern door to door as I shouted smugly, "Trick or treat!" My sisters made fun of my self-importance and kept running ahead, leaving me behind.

They're just jealous, I thought.

They ran over some railroad tracks into a neighborhood we didn't know that well. I was struggling to keep up, yelling out, "Hey, you guys, wait for me!" when I tripped over a lawn sprinkler. As I went down, the cheap plastic strap on the jack-o'-lantern snapped off. My precious pumpkin head full of treats was suddenly spinning wildly through the air, candy shooting out over the grass like sparks from a twirling firecracker. I grabbed the broken jack-o'-lantern and frantically scooped up my treats, pleading with my sisters to help me.

Could this get any worse? I wondered.

Unfortunately, the answer was yes. I sniffed my hands and discovered that I'd been scooping up dog poop with my candy! My sisters laughed and ran away as I remained on my knees, now desperate to get my hands clean. My whole Halloween had turned into a smelly mess.

Later that night, my mother made my sisters share their candy with me, which they did grudgingly, giving me the second-rate stuff that no one likes.

My beloved jack-o'-lantern had let me down. Halloween was never the same again.

TERESA STANLEY · TULARE, CA

Teresa and Tracey always wore hobo masks on Halloween. Older sister Margaret went as Casper.

COSTUMED KIDS

HORSING AROUND

As an amateur photographer, I took hundreds of slides of my family through the 1960s and 1970s. In this picture taken in 1964, my two children dressed up as a stallion for a special event.
BRUCE THOMPSON
WAUKESHA, WI

SNAP, CRACKLE, POP!

For every Halloween parade in Bellefonte, Pennsylvania, our mother, Barbara Korman, made us costumes based on a threesome theme. Jeff (left), Jack (right) and I won silver dollars each year. Here we are in 1964.
JOYCE WILKES
EDINBORO, PA

KITCHEN CARVER

Holiday tradition in our house meant that I carved the turkey. Here, getting directives from my wife, Joyce, I buzz into the bird with an electric knife—state-of-the-art equipment in 1965.

BRUCE THOMPSON · WAUKESHA, WI

When I was growing up in the '40s, my mother always made Thanksgiving dinner for my grandparents. While she prepared the meal, my dad took me and my brother to see the Thanksgiving Day parade in downtown Detroit, Michigan, which ended with Santa Claus waving to the crowds.

GEORGIA BROWNE · STURGIS, MI

UP NORTH IN THE PINK STATION WAGON

AUTOMOBILES TODAY ARE a marvel of technology and ingenuity. But I was raised during a simpler time. We had one car—a large pink Oldsmobile station wagon. The car wasn't awarded to us by Mary Kay but rather was chosen by my father out of necessity. Despite the color, the car had to haul five children and their parents all around western Minnesota, with holiday trips to visit grandparents in northern Minnesota.

The Olds had no seat belts, no air bags, no rear cameras and no warning alarms. We could count on two minimally effective safety features: 1. The car was built like a large pink tank, and 2. My mother.

With her maternal urge to protect her flock from head-on crashes, deer suddenly darting across the road, and the Russians unleashing the Big One on Middle America, my mother developed her own safety feature called "Hit the floor."

Although we never had to use it in an actual emergency, we practiced it frequently on trips to the Iron Range. There were no electronics involved, just the no-nonsense tone of Mom's voice yelling, "Hit the floor!"

No matter who was on your lap, who called shotgun or who had the enviable position by the window, five children, ranging in age from 2 to 14, dove for the floorboards, hoping to not be the one left on top to face the impending disaster. After all, we were still children and the world revolved around us.

I often wonder if our mom's strategy for using this device had another purpose on those seemingly endless trips to our grandparents' homes. Five antsy kids, packed in a car for three hours, would make a natural plot for a really scary movie. With parents on their last nerve, sisters bickering about the little brother touching them, the kids not having enough space to spread out, and one or more of us being hungry, tired or thirsty, the clamor eventually became too much to bear, and Mom would yell, "Hit the floor!"

All petty bickering stopped instantly as we scrambled for the floorboards, wondering what would happen next. The Olds was quiet while we awaited word to get back in our seats.

One time I peeked at Mom, who had a smirk on her face, and noticed a grateful nod from Dad, whose neck was red and pulsing.

When the Olds pulled into the driveway, all four doors flew open and, as if the car were a disturbed anthill, its occupants poured out. The fleeting look of panic on our grandparents' faces was soon replaced by smiles, hugs and kisses. Then we nearly knocked them over, racing inside to see what graced the dining table. Sure enough, a golden, magazine-worthy turkey, mounds of mashed potatoes, luscious brown gravy and a sideboard piled high with pies were enough to appease everyone.

SHERI SMITH
PONSFORD, MN

TO MARKET, TO MARKET, TO BUY A FAT TURKEY

ON THE TUESDAY BEFORE Thanksgiving 1932, Grandfather, Mother, my cousin Jack and I went on a special shopping trip in Oakland, California—not just down to East 14th Street, but all the way downtown to the big farmers market below 10th and Broadway.

Off we went, Jack and I running and hopping, down the street to catch good ol' No. 11. The trolley car came clanking and banging down the hill and hissed to a stop at our corner. We scrambled up the steps and Grandfather put four trolley tokens in the glass holder for all of us.

The motorman stomped his foot on the warning bell and, with his right hand, pulled the lever that snapped the doors shut. With a jerk and a start, the trolley zoomed down the hill.

Grandfather knew the motorman, so when the car wasn't crowded he stood and talked with him for a short time, bracing himself against the brass rail. I was glad when he sat down. A sign read: "All passengers MUST be seated when the trolley is in motion," and my cousin told me Grandfather could get in trouble if he didn't sit down.

I loved to ride the trolley! Our car, Trolley No. 11, sped along, careening around curves and slowing down as it went up the side of a hill. We whizzed past the movie house, Montgomery Ward, the hospital, assorted shops and the shores of Lake Merritt.

At last we passed the courthouse and rounded the corner. There was the Tribune Tower, for many years the tallest building around. It had a clock that could be seen for miles when it was lit up at night. Just as we passed the tower, Grandfather reached up and pulled the cord, and the trolley ground to a screeching stop. We scrambled off in a hurry.

The farmers market was big, and I never really liked it much. I was always afraid I'd get lost. There were huge open archways with iron gates to close them off at night. The tile floor was nearly always damp from being hosed down. Stalls for vegetables and fruit lined one wall. Cut flowers and potted plants ran along another wall. Down the center stood counters and places to buy drinks and food. At the far end of the market were the fish, chicken, rabbit and turkey sellers.

On our first stop, Grandfather picked out a turkey from a truckful out back. He looked over the birds carefully and pointed to the one he deemed best. He made arrangements to have it dressed and delivered to the house early the next day.

Then we went to the fish market. That was more fun because it didn't smell as bad. There were bins full of crabs crawling all over each other and waving their claws. There were big fish, little fish, squid with their odd-looking tendrils, and baskets of oysters and shrimp. Grandfather always picked out one—a large crab, some shrimp or oysters—but never all three.

The next stop was the fruit and vegetable stalls for fresh cranberries, pearl onions, and cauliflower or Brussels sprouts.

At a dairy stall, we bought butter and cream. The bags were full now and it was time to go—but not before Grandfather bought some good white wine. My mother bought some peppermints and perhaps a few apples or an orange or two. Mother and Grandfather each carried black leather shopping bags, now bulging and heavy.

We forged our way through the throngs of people. The marketplace was noisy, with everyone shouting to make themselves heard. Children were everywhere. Big sisters with baby brothers and bright-eyed boys, noses pressed against the glass counters of pastries and candies.

There seemed to be people of every ethnicity and age: ancient Chinese gentlemen in long garments with beards, middle-aged Chinese women in black jackets and slippers with big pins in their hair, Swedish sailors with watch caps, and Italians and Portuguese. Grandfather spoke Portuguese, Italian and Swedish.

Soon we were boarding the No. 11 for the trip home.

Wednesday morning the pies were made, and Jack and I polished the silver. Then we folded napkins and did other chores to keep us busy. The table was set and the centerpiece arranged. One year it was a horn of plenty, another year an Indian canoe with flowers. We made place cards using walnut shells with little sails for names.

In those days, schools closed for the week of Thanksgiving, allowing people to be with their families for a longer period of time or to travel to one another's homes, if necessary. The holiday was truly an event.

MAE ELIZABETH LOCKWOOD
OAKLAND, CA

Rolling Through the Years

Many hands make short work
of treasured ravioli recipe.

———

My mom and dad started the tradition of making raviolis more than 50 years ago, with my brother, sister and me helping out. We always made them on Christmas Day. After getting up early and opening our presents, we'd march into the kitchen and start the preparations for the special meal. Sometimes, as soon as we finished cleaning up, the doorbell would ring, announcing our company.

For a few years we made raviolis one week for Dad's family and the next week for Mom's family, but that didn't last very long—it was too much work. We just invited both sides of the family for one big meal.

The family recipe came from my maternal grandmother, Mary Saccaro, who learned it from her mother. The recipe had been handed down from mother to daughter for many generations in Sicily and carried over to Chicago, Illinois, when Grandma Saccaro's family arrived in the late 19th century.

Grandma never measured anything; it was all done by intuition. The recipe wasn't even written down until the early 1960s, when Grandma was making raviolis one last time to celebrate the birth of a granddaughter, and there was a danger we would lose the knowledge. My mother and several of my aunts measured and recorded the amounts whenever Grandma called for "a pinch" of this and "a handful" of that. When we tried the recipe the following year, we agreed the raviolis were as good as Grandma's had been.

Before we started the pasta, Mom made a red sauce of canned tomatoes, garlic, basil and oregano. She added Italian sausage, pork neck bones and homemade meatballs. Our sauce—we never called it "gravy," as the characters on *The Sopranos* referred to tomato sauce—simmered for hours; we basked in the aroma while we labored over the raviolis.

We sat around the kitchen table in an assembly line, flattening and turning the dough balls with the rolling pin. We'd fill the flattened dough with cheese, seal the dumplings with a shot glass, and crimp the edges with a fork.

Anyone who needed a break would take the finished raviolis from the kitchen table to the drying sheet in the bedroom, keeping a running tally of our production.

We never rolled out the dough with a pasta machine when I was a kid; we did it by hand to get the consistency just right. Everybody took turns with the rolling pin because it was a hard job. You could get fired or demoted if your rolling method wasn't up to Mom's standards. I should know—I've been demoted several times.

The yearly task of ravioli-making became a time to bond as we told stories about all the relatives and teased each other about past cooking mistakes. Nothing interfered with the process. Two weeks after my dad died, we still gathered in the kitchen, and making the raviolis helped us get through the grief as a family.

Over the years, spouses and grandchildren have joined the crew. We've also gotten high-tech: Now we grate the cheese with a hand-crank grater—no more skinned knuckles!—and start the flattening of the dough balls with a pasta machine, though we still finish rolling them by hand.

Today we make the raviolis a week in advance and freeze them, instead of getting up early on Christmas Day, but Mom still makes sure we follow Grandma Saccaro's original recipe to the letter. Our raviolis are as tasty as they were when we began the tradition.

FRANK C. MODICA
URBANA, IL

HELPING HANDS

We all did our part to help our grandma Lillian Stawarky fix the feast. We polished pans, mashed turnips and potatoes, and made cookies out of leftover pie crust. After dinner, we went downtown to see the holiday lights. My dad, Vin, took this photo in 1963. I'm third from the left in the back.

MIKE SIMKO
BRIDGEPORT, CT

MASTER DECORATORS

I fondly recall holiday baking with my kids Susan and Danny. Danny is sprinkling a paintbrush, which he used to decorate the cookies. This picture was taken in 1954 at our family's home in Madison, Wisconsin.

KAY SCHOPP · TUCSON, AZ

Multiple Layers of Paint

This cherished heirloom has survived five generations.

────

My mother, Marjorie Martin Mangrum, was from a family in Williamson County, Tennessee. Her grandfather B.C. Wilkes was a woodworker and made beautiful caskets and custom cabinetry.

In the fall of 1928, when my mom was 7, she visited her grandfather's workshop. She watched as he lovingly built a pint-sized china cabinet. She later told me how she wished that cabinet could be hers.

Her grandfather told her it was for a little girl who lived down the road. Imagine my mother's delight when she found the miniature piece of furniture under the Christmas tree that year.

Fast-forward to Christmas morning 1950. I found the same cabinet with a fresh coat of paint under our Christmas tree. My baby sister was born that year, and we spent countless happy hours playing house with our grown-up kitchen cabinet.

In 1966 and 1969, I had my own daughters. I replaced the cabinet's knobs and repainted it so my girls could use the piece in their playhouse.

My daughters had girls of their own, and every time they visited Granny's house, the first thing they wanted to play with was the little cabinet.

Now I have a great-granddaughter, Makayla, and whenever she stays with me she has a fun time playing outside with the storage unit she calls her kitchen.

I'm sure B.C. Wilkes never dreamed that five generations of little girls would continue the tradition of playing with the petite piece he built with love so many years ago.

Christmas 1950 brought Melba, top, plenty of fun playthings. Melba's great-granddaughter, Makayla, above, keeps up the family tradition.

MELBA BROWN
OLMSTEAD, KY

AN ADVERTISING VETERAN

Though St. Nick appeared in ads in 1840, it wasn't until after 1863, when cartoonist Thomas Nast created the now-familiar figure in a red suit with a white beard, that Santa became the holiday season's most popular pitchman.

1972 »

Yule Love This Salesman

In this ad from *Better Homes & Gardens*, Santa pitches the Sweet Story Book as a last-minute "life saver."

≫ 1962

Santa Suds

In *Family Circle*, Colgate's Soaky Santa bath suds was a popular stocking stuffer, and a toy when the bottle was empty.

« 1962

Kris Kringle Cold Calls

From *Family Circle*, Santa gives everyone's favorite condiment—long before Del Monte conceded to calling it ketchup in the '80s.

THE JOY OF CHRISTMAS

NONSTOP SMILE

Here I am as a 6-year-old, hugging a doll on Christmas morning 1956 while showing off my gappy grin. Only eight years earlier, Spike Jones and His City Slickers recorded "All I Want for Christmas Is My Two Front Teeth," which became a Billboard hit and has remained a popular holiday novelty song all these years. Several artists have recorded their own version, including George Strait, Nat King Cole and Jimmy Buffett.
LYNETTE JEAN GIBBONEY
COLUMBUS, OH

THE BIG HAUL

In December 1960, a friend and I paid $2 for a pair of pines we cut ourselves at a Michigan farm, and then we drove back to Chicago. We must have looked like a bush going down the highway in my '57 Chevrolet.
WARREN KOSTELNY · MOUNT PROSPECT, IL

GRATEFUL KIDS

What's Christmas without a fireplace, even if it is cardboard? My children, from left, Kevin, Gregory, Paula and Kathleen, show off their Christmas gifts in 1966.

BARBARA MOHR
MILLINGTON, MI

CHRISTMAS CAME AT LAST

Our military family lived in Germany and was scheduled to return to America in December 1954. Mom had shipped our Christmas gifts to our grandparents' house in Evansville, Indiana. But our return was delayed, and my younger brother, David, 4, and I worried that Santa would never find us. Mom bought us a few small presents and made us picture books of all the things Santa had delivered to Indiana. When we finally arrived in February, our grandparents Vernie and Stella Jones (above) had a fully decorated tree waiting for us. We had the best Christmas ever.

ROBERTA SHARP · MOORESVILLE, IN

SANTA'S SECRET

Even though I could not speak English then (1945), I was so excited to see Sani Closi, as we called him in Italian, in Santa Cruz, California.

NORMA WILSON
SCOTTS VALLEY, CA

Celebrating Grandma's birthday in 1949, Arlene sits with her doll and Grandma Elizabeth Scott.

All Aglow in Lights

Grandma's birthday was the final hurrah.

Little Christmas, also known as Epiphany, was nearly as special as Christmas when I was growing up in the 1940s in Iron River, Michigan. On Jan. 6, all my relatives got together to celebrate my grandmother's birthday and take down her Christmas tree with her. Sometimes my aunts, uncles and cousins from as far as Marquette, Michigan (almost 90 miles away), would come for a visit.

We cousins were allowed to carefully remove the special ornaments from the tree. I remember them well, especially two wooden Easter eggs given to Grandma by a neighbor girl who went to college—a big deal in our small town. Grandma tied ribbons around them and turned them into ornaments.

The ornaments were carefully wrapped in tissue paper and packed in a box that was stored behind a curtain in Grandma's closet until the week before Christmas the following year. In those days, we never put up decorations any earlier than a week before Christmas. It just wasn't right.

Some years I helped Grandma make paper chains from construction paper to decorate the tree (those we threw away). Once, we made popcorn-and-cranberry chains, but we didn't try that again because it was too hard to run the needle and thread through the popcorn without breaking it and pricking our fingers.

Taking Grandma's special sugar cookies off the tree was the best part of the event. By early January the cookies were pretty stale, but to us kids they were still delicious. We felt very grown up eating cookies and drinking coffee with the adults. Of course, our coffee was diluted with canned milk and sugar.

Uncle John also bought a special birthday cake at the A&P store. Grandma couldn't be expected to bake her own birthday cake.

We sat in her living room, turned on the tree lights and basked in their glow one last time, enjoying the stale Christmas cookies, store-bought birthday cake and coffee.

The final step was to remove the lights from the tree. It was always a little sad being tucked into bed that night, knowing it wouldn't be Christmas again for another whole year.

But that wasn't the end. The next morning my uncles hauled Grandma's tree outdoors, where my older cousins and their friends placed it on the hill and covered it with snow. Their makeshift ski jump lasted until about March, when the snow melted.

ARLENE SHOVALD · SALIDA, CO

Joyous Noel

In 1960, the year I turned 5, my family celebrated Christmas in Karlsruhe, Germany, where my father, Gabby, an engineer, worked for the Singer sewing machine company. My older sister, Phyrne, 13, loved stuffed animals as much as I did. My mom, Fernanda, took the photo.

PHYLLIS GEBHARDT · KISSIMMEE, FL

CHAPTER 10

LAST LAUGH

Who doesn't love a good laugh?
Delight in these silly situations and good
fun—after all, a smile is universal.

Be a Clown

Members of the Mills Bros. Circus, this clown troupe
traveled from the East Coast to the Midwest with a stop
in Janesville, Wisconsin, on July 3, 1950.

Dressed for church, from left, are Dede's mom, Ellen Marston, sister Polly and her mother-in-law, Mabel Wilson.

Oh, She Can Help You

Look-alike servers confuse the congregation.

The Rev. Franklin Parker (a legend among area folks) and his wife, our Aunt Al, were host and hostess for the Saturday evening Baked Bean Suppers sponsored by the Chichester Congregational Church in Chichester, New Hampshire, many years ago.

When we were teenagers, my sister, Polly, and I often pitched in and waited on tables. In spite of a three-year difference in our ages, many people, Mom included, had trouble telling us apart. Once, we decided to dress alike and confuse folks at our tables. Whenever someone asked one of us for something from the kitchen, we responded, "I'll tell my sister. She's assigned to your table." Much to our delight, it worked.

Aunt Al smiled and shook her head at us, realizing what we were up to. She glanced around the room to make sure everything was in order before heading back to lend a hand in the kitchen. She knew our prank was harmless.

The busy room hummed with eager voices. Rev. Parker welcomed regulars and newcomers

Dede, Polly's look-alike, poses with a mischievous look in her eye.

alike. We placed platters of potato salad trimmed with sprigs of parsley on the tables. We filled water glasses and took orders for coffee or iced tea. When we brought out the steaming bowls of baked beans and baskets of soft rolls, conversation suspended for a short while. Hearty eaters dipped into their second helpings as the clock slowly ticked away.

Dessert consisted of apple, pumpkin, lemon meringue, custard and cherry pies, along with an assortment of cakes. Two, even three helpings of pie and cake made their way to the tables along with refills of coffee.

Finally, those at the tables pushed back their chairs, slipped on their wraps and got up to leave, uttering sincere promises to come again.

With a surge of activity, Polly and I hurried to reset the tables as more people crowded in for their supper. As we delivered more food, a light breeze stirred the tablecloths.

DEDE HAMMOND · ZEPHYRHILLS, FL

Pardon the Pantyhose

Nothing to see below the waist.

To make some extra money in 1986 when my son was small, I started selling Avon products part time. I was really shy about it, but I needed the money. I slowly expanded my territory and tried to reach as many neighbors and acquaintances as possible.

I always tried to look my best while on my route and wore my good casual clothes and jewelry. I had only a few pairs of dress slacks, so when I got home I removed them along with my pantyhose and hung them up.

I worked for five years and found the people I visited truly enjoyable. One woman had a physical condition making it difficult for her to walk, but she never seemed to let it get her down. When I went to her house, she called from her chair to let me in.

One day I was rushing to get my orders delivered and I got dressed rather quickly. I grabbed all my sacks of perfume and cosmetics and arrived at the woman's house with her purchase. We had a good visit and, as usual, she made me laugh.

When I let myself out, her tiny dog followed, grabbing at my pant leg as I closed the door. I tried to ignore it, but the dog started growling and fussing as if I was some sort of prey. I was about to panic when I saw the dog shaking something. I looked down to find that it had my pantyhose in its mouth.

I burst out laughing. It seems I had put on my slacks without noticing that my hose was still inside one leg. The dog saw it and attacked as if it was an animal or foreign object.

I sheepishly went back inside to show my customer what had happened. She had heard the commotion and wondered what was going on. She found the whole thing amusing.

I was embarrassed, to say the least, but ever since that incident, I've made sure that no dryer sheet, clean laundry or pantyhose is left inside my pants before I put them on. Let's call it my pantyhose phobia.

ANGELINE STONER
FLORAL, AR

The Mystery of the Disappearing Forks

Mom couldn't get her count quite right.

———

As the lab director at a hospital, my dad always had his employees come to our house for various seasonal parties. On the day of the party, Mom would be busy cleaning, decorating and setting the table. Her place settings were intricate, with the napkins all in a row and beside each plate a precise semicircle of forks. It was a tricky operation that required all of her concentration.

On one of these occasions, my sister Linda and I were supposed to be helping Mom. Even these many years later, I have no explanation for what happened next. It was as if Linda and I were of one mind. We looked at each other and smiled. We executed our plan perfectly, as if we had rehearsed it many times instead of just dreaming it up on the spot.

Coming back from the kitchen with silverware in hand, Mom set about lining up the forks with the efficiency of a general. She counted them and decided that she needed more, so back to the kitchen she went.

Then Linda struck: She swept up several forks and casually made her way to the kitchen. As our sweet mother returned with more forks, she passed Linda, who was on her way to deposit the stolen ones back in the drawer. Mom, puzzled, stared at the table and very carefully counted again—and went back to the kitchen for more forks. We repeated the trick flawlessly at least three more times.

Finally, we couldn't contain our laughter any longer and told Mom what we had done. I think she was so relieved she wasn't going crazy that she didn't have time to be mad at us.

PATTY BALLARD · LAKE WORTH, FL

MERRILY THEY ROLLED ALONG THEIR MALTED MILKY WAY

DURING THE BUSY CHRISTMAS SEASON in 1972, I worked at J.C. Penney selling luggage and greeting cards.

It was the custom that sales associates would fill in for clerks from different departments who were taking their breaks. When my turn came, I relieved the candy clerk. I hated working the candy counter because you had to weigh every ounce of candy manually to calculate the cost.

Every day, the candy department featured two specials loaded in bins at each end of the counter. Malted milk balls were one of the specials that day. My first customer asked for a quarter-ounce of them. I opened the bin, but realized too late I'd used the wrong door. Malted milk balls spilled out faster than coins from a slot machine, bouncing loudly onto the floor and rolling everywhere.

Several customers had lined up, and I was ankle deep in malted milk balls. I tottered in my high heels, murdering milk balls— *crunch! crunch!*—as I struggled to remain upright while trying to serve everyone.

Just then, the regular candy clerk returned from her break, and seeing my predicament, burst out laughing. The two of us scooped up the runaway candy as fast as we could. We may have eaten one or two (or 10)—purely in the interest of cleanup, of course. I kept thinking of that *I Love Lucy* episode where Lucy and Ethel can't keep up with the conveyor belt of chocolates at the candy factory.

After that, I was very happy to return to luggage and greeting cards, where no one could order a quarter-ounce of anything.

CONNIE CHRISTENSEN
WEST ALLIS, WI

CURLS ARE OVERRATED

FIVE IN MY FAMILY HAD RED HAIR—THREE SIBLINGS, my father and myself. Our tresses were torched at birth with a variety of tones ranging from flaming to auburn to strawberry blond. Our locks were exceptionally straight and ideal for a cut called a Dutch-boy bob. Mother found the look convenient because brushing our hair meant no tangles, snags or tussles.

Then, life changed with the birth of my sister Margaret Louise, or Peggy for short.

Peggy's blond hair fell in waves, with a natural curl that cascaded down the right side of her chubby little face. The attention she got was nothing short of terrifying for her older sister, me.

As a 4-year-old in 1935, I had more than a pinch of creativity. To hone my skills, I imagined Peggy without her curl. Furthermore, I knew just the tool to fulfill my creative urge.

"Peggy," I asked, with a hint of excitement in my voice, "do you want to play beauty shop?"

"Yeth," came her toothy reply.

The stool was handy, so I placed her on it. I found large kitchen scissors in the catch-all drawer and set about my role as beautician. Up came the curl and snap went the scissors. I soon took care of the red-ribboned bow as well.

The next thing I remember hearing was my mother closing the front door and entering the room. Immediately after that came the sound of my bottom being spanked.

In spite of this, Peggy has never mentioned this story. Could it be that she was too young to recall? I have always hoped so.

PATRICIA EDWARDS
LAKEWOOD, CA

Peggy's adorable curls were the envy of all her siblings, big sister Patricia, at right, included.

An Accidental Volley in the Cold War

On the road to discovery, his experiment backfired.

Born in Washington, D.C., less than a year before the Cuban missile crisis in 1962, I grew up when the fear of getting bombed by the Soviets was extremely pervasive.

At age 3, my favorite place to sit in the whole car was on the hump in the front floorboard so I could watch Dad work the pedals on our big Chrysler. This was before mandatory child seats,

and my mother thought I was as safe down there as anywhere else.

That's where I was sitting one day in February 1965. We were heading away from downtown on Rock Creek Parkway. A storm had struck the night before, burdening tree branches with ice. Ahead of us was a car with four men wearing furry Cossack hats. Dad guessed they were from the Russian embassy and kept his distance. The last thing he wanted was to skid on a patch of ice and ram into them.

The Russians gave their turn signal as we approached Massachusetts Avenue. It's a long ramp, so we were driving parallel to them for several feet. Dad glanced at the Russians, who glanced back.

Meanwhile, I had become transfixed by Dad's keys dangling from the ignition. It suddenly dawned on me that they somehow made the car go. To test my theory, I reached through Dad's legs and turned the ignition key.

The Chrysler lurched wildly. Dad quickly realized the problem and shifted into neutral to restart, but not before the engine sucked in carbureted gasoline, which exploded inside the muffler in a string of bursts that sounded like a machine gun going off.

All four furry Cossack hats vanished as the Russians ducked to save their lives from the crazy Americans firing on them. Their car left the road, spun 360 degrees on some ice and, amazingly, righted itself back onto the ramp. They continued on their way without a look back. And so did we. But now, against my will, I was on the seat.

JONATHAN WALTER
WARSAW, IN

INTERMISSION STAMPEDE

DRIVE-IN THEATERS WERE all the rage from the 1950s to the mid-'80s. Both my mom and dad had full-time jobs and also worked part time at a local drive-in.

I learned how to fix things to help at home. When I turned 16, I got a job at the area's largest outdoor theater, the Lincoln Drive-In on U.S. Route 1 just outside of Philadelphia, Pennsylvania, and my fix-it skills came with me. I did whatever my boss asked, tearing tickets, parking cars and repairing speakers and in-car heaters—even breaking up the occasional fistfight on the field.

At intermission one night, the manager asked me to leave my post at the snack counter and fix the jammed dime machine in the ladies room. She also handed me a package of the machine's contents in case I couldn't fix it fast enough.

My face turned as red as a chili pepper and sweat beaded on my brow. But she gave me that look, so I charged forward to save the day.

I was met by a group of women holding dimes, which I quickly exchanged for product, stuffing the coins into my pocket. I fumbled with the machine, opening and unjamming it. Once I fixed it, I tested it, topped off the contents and closed the door to a thunderous round of applause.

As I turned to walk out, the women actually opened a path for me. I felt like royalty.

WAYNE MOYER
MIDLOTHIAN, VA

With the advent of car culture, new places opened wherever families could drive.

PRIME-TIME CEREALS

How morning food became an anytime snack.

"Me and my big heart"

1955 »

Rockwell Sells

In the mid-'50s, Norman Rockwell drew a series of delightful portraits of freckled boys and pigtailed girls to promote Kellogg's Corn Flakes, transforming the venerable brand into a children's favorite. This ad from *Life* shows the cereal as a quick meal kids can prepare themselves.

"Any choice of cereals tempts <u>any</u> family ...as long as it's from **Post-Tens**"

A choice for all ages—that's Post-Tens. Eight different, delicious cereals—including new Post Alpha-Bits—in ten separate individual boxes. Have fun! Let your family pick and choose their favorites from Post-Tens!

"ALL POST CEREALS HAPPEN TO BE JUST A LITTLE BIT BETTER"

« 1958

Kid-Sized for Fun

Post answered competitor Kellogg's Rockwell campaign with ads from another *Saturday Evening Post* illustrator, Richard "Dick" Sargent, whose style was more obviously tongue-in-cheek. This scene of kids playing grown-ups at an afternoon tea party with snack-size Post-Tens is classic Sargent, rich in humorous detail. Note that "Dad" is too young to read—the newspaper is upside down.

Do Look Behind That Curtain

Her shower stunt dripped with irony.

———

Back in 1965, when I was 13, I came home from a baby-sitting job to an empty house. My parents and brother were at church, and my sister was at work. I went into the bathroom and peeled off my clothes to take a shower. Just then, I heard my sister come home. I decided this was the perfect opportunity to scare her, so I hid behind the shower curtain to lunge out when she passed by. But instead of coming in, she dropped everything and ran out the door. *Sheesh! What's wrong with her?* I wondered. I shrugged it off and took my shower.

Unfortunately, I was in for a nasty shock of my own. Without realizing it, I *had* frightened my sister: She'd heard the shower curtain rustling, seen my clothes and thought the worst. She jumped back into her car, sped to church and burst into the service shouting, "There's someone in the house, and I saw Janet's clothes on the floor!" My family bolted from the church, believing that something terrible had happened to me. Dad was speeding, so a cop pulled him over. After Dad told him the situation, the police officer followed him home.

The next thing I knew, my entire family and the policeman were running in to see if I was OK. I was forced to explain to everyone that there had been no intruder, I'd just been hiding in the shower to scare my sister. Talk about embarrassing. To make matters worse, everyone from church dropped by later that evening, one by painful one, to make sure I was all right.

That was the first—and last—time I ever tried to pull a prank on my sister.

JANET INGRAM · LOVELAND, CO

A TAIL OF ADVENTURE

MY COUSIN KENNY CALLED FROM THE FARM.
"Why don't you get someone to bring you up here? I want to teach you how to ride a goat."

Kenny usually had some questionable scheme going, and this latest one sounded like more fun than waiting for Grandpa's pipe to go out so I could light it.

"I'll be there as soon as I can," I told him.

When I got there, Kenny was ready with a goat tied to a tree. "If you want to turn right, reach back and pull his tail to the left," he explained. "The same if you want him to go left, tail to the right. It's easy."

I wasn't so sure, but since I was already on the animal, I was beyond the point of changing my mind. Kenny loosened the tie and the goat took off in an instant, heading straight for a barbed wire fence. I was desperately trying to grab his tail to get him to turn right, but I never found it before we crashed.

Kenny was running after us and pulled me off the fence, while the poor goat managed to escape to the barn. All that was left for me to do was wonder how I would explain my torn and bloodstained clothes to my mother.

I think I've had more respect for all animals ever since that adventure.

ROBERT JOHNSON · FOREST CITY, IA

HORSING AROUND

GROWING UP ON AN IOWA FARM offered my sisters and me many excellent opportunities to be imaginative and inventive. We were always outdoors because our parents believed that we should stay out of their way or work.

We taught our pony, Billy, to do a few tricks, including a special one, playing dead. Unfortunately, he also quickly learned that if he fell over and played dead while we were riding him, we would get off his back, which Billy preferred. Playing dead became his favorite trick.

Once, while at a horse show, Billy stretched out in his dead mode and refused to get up. With no chairs available, my dad simply sat on Billy's shoulder. A woman walking by was horrified that this big man had "killed that little pony!"

I am sure that I saw our Billy smile.

SUSAN HELLERT
DUBUQUE, IA

We taught our pony, Billy, to do a few tricks.

Revenge Is a
Dish Best Served Cold

Wife made sure she got the last laugh.

M y wife, Mary, was a probation officer in Scott County, Iowa, and I had recently launched my own trucking company, starting with one used dump truck.

We learned of an old fixer-upper farmhouse out in the country with rent so cheap it defied logic, so we jumped at it. Built during World War II, the house had no insulation, and the antiquated oil furnace had no fan to circulate the heat. If the wind was blowing, you'd have to hold your hat tight on your head while seated at the kitchen table. Winters were a challenge.

One day, I was working on a replacement truck engine in the basement of the house when I heard Mary running the vacuum just above me in the living room. The floor was so thin I could tell exactly where she was in the room.

As she worked her way to the far end, I unscrewed the fuse that powered the wall sockets, and the sweeper stopped. Mary walked over to the socket, I screwed the fuse back in, and the sweeper started up again. She walked back to the sweeper, and I again unscrewed the fuse. Back to the wall she went, this time with what sounded like an expression of frustration. By the third round, Mary let fly a barrage of embarrassing language that told the sweeper it was on its way to the junkyard.

I could no longer contain myself. She heard me laughing and figured it out. Mary, who has a wonderful sense of humor, laughed, too. But she never forgot.

Not long after, still deep in winter, I was taking a bath in our frigid bathroom with only the warmth of the bathwater for comfort. The door opened

and in came Mary carrying a 5-gallon bucket of icy water. She calmly reminded me of the sweeper episode. *Oh no.*

"Please, Mary, don't. Please!"

She dumped the entire contents on me, then sweetly asked, "Who's laughing now?"

JAMES ORR
DAVENPORT, IA

The Aqua-Nuts you can see are, from left, Steve Argentieri, Bill Remington, Wilson "Whitey" Hagadorn and Joe Solo. Also in the troupe were Eddy Rawady, Dave Generalli and Bud Baker.

On the March for Fun

When it came to comedy, they all knew the drill.

M y father, Joe, belonged to a troupe called the Aqua-Nuts Comedy Drill Team, which performed in parades and sporting events throughout western New York and Pennsylvania in the 1960s. Formed by local funnyman Eddy Rawady, the Aqua-Nuts enjoyed some fame during the seven or eight years they were together.

Their uniforms were old-timey bathing suits made by their wives, high-top sneakers colored in a checkerboard pattern, white work gloves and tricorn hats worn backward. They carried ceremonial guns cut and fashioned from two-by-fours, painted white, with pieces of black rubber hose glued on to form the barrels. In every parade, Rawady would lead the Nuts pushing a huge sword on wheels with a cornstalk poking out of his hat.

Each of the guys has a favorite story from their many performances. One of their fondest memories is appearing at the annual grape and wine festival in Naples, New York, in 1966 or '67. Sen. Robert Kennedy, D-N.Y., was there prior to his campaign for president, and sent word to the troupe how much he enjoyed their show.

The memory that brings the biggest laugh, however, has to do with a woman who approached them after a parade in Hornell, New York, where they were based. As they were heading over to the American Legion, she asked them where they lived. When they told her, she replied that they were a disgrace to the Hornell community.

They've been laughing about it ever since. Except for that one woman, everyone they met loved the Aqua-Nuts, who in turn loved to make people laugh.

FRAN SOLO
ENDICOTT, NY

SHE WORE THE BURLAP IN THE FAMILY

BURLAP MAY NOT BE THE textile of choice for garments, but my mother wore it like a banner one day to teach our dad a lesson.

In 1955, Dad was a machinist with a company in Coffeyville, Kansas, about 100 miles from our home in the Ozarks. He rented a room during the week and came home on weekends.

The company published its own magazine, with the occasional short profile of an employee. The May issue that year featured my father and his many adventures–panning for gold in Canada, appearing in silent movies with the actress Mary Astor, operating a motel.

Conspicuously absent was any mention of his family. Miffed, Mom quipped that "it all sounded like a bachelor on the loose," then added ominously, "someday they'll find out about your family."

When she learned Dad's company was holding its annual picnic at the city fairgrounds, Mom decided to make good on her threat. Using burlap bags from the feed store, she made dresses for herself and my sister Gerry and baggy loincloths for my brother Jim and me. Boy, did that burlap sure itch! She also packed tobacco from a crumpled cigarette into a souvenir corncob pipe.

It was a warm day in June when we reached the fairgrounds, where hundreds of company employees and their families were relaxing after lunch. Mom lit the pipe, bent over like an old crone and clomped off with the three of us trailing behind her like burlap-covered ducklings. The stunned crowd parted. Tongues froze midair over melting ice cream cones. I was only 5, but I remember wondering what I'd done to deserve this.

Holding the company magazine open to Dad's picture, Mom marched up to a group of picnickers and demanded in an exaggerated drawl, "Have you'ns seen this here feller anywhere?"

Someone pointed at the registration booth, and we spotted him with some other men, one of whom was the plant supervisor. On cue, we all ran up to him and did as Mom had instructed: We threw our arms around him and yelled "Pappy! Pappy!" Dad looked shocked, and then burst out laughing. The company president laughed, too, and a few minutes later, he had us all pose with him for pictures for the next magazine.

RICHARD ALBINS
CROSSVILLE, TN

MYSTERY DISH SOUNDS TASTY

MAMA MARRIED DADDY JACK,
a sergeant in the Army Air Corps, in 1941, when I was almost 4, and we all moved to a military base near Las Vegas, Nevada.

Mornings I liked to sit under the table with my paper dolls while Mama and Daddy Jack talked and drank their coffee. One morning I heard Mama say, "Oh Jack, I don't know how to make ends meet this week."

Oh no, I thought, *Mama doesn't know how to make insmeat.* She'd never made it before, but suddenly I so badly wanted to try it. My mouth was watering for some delicious insmeat.

A few days later some neighbor ladies were over for morning coffee. I was in my usual spot under the table, playing with my paper dolls and still thinking about Mama's cooking dilemma.

I crawled up on a chair and blurted out, "Mrs. Hoffman, can you tell Mama how to make insmeat?"

There was silence for several seconds and then they all laughed.

"No one can," one lady said.

"Ask Uncle Sam!" another joked.

Uncle Sam—who's he? Another mystery to solve.

NORMI DOUGLASS · WACO, TX

Normi worried about Mom's culinary skills.

HITTING THE HIGH LIFE

On Halloween nights in my hometown of Grand Ledge, Michigan, starting in 1958, my dad would climb onto the roof of his '54 Pontiac and transform in front of our eyes. He attached stilts to his legs, donned a long-tailed black coat and walked the streets in high fashion. He made the stilts from two lengths of wood, attached work boots at the bottom and draped faded curtain fabric to resemble pants. With a black top hat on his graying pate, black-rimmed glasses and a big red nose, Dad created a character everyone loved.

One year, the manager of the Sun Theatre asked him to replace the burned-out bulbs in the theater's billboard marquee. Dad was so talented, and he was committed to entertaining kids as well as adults.

DOUGLAS MAXSON · CEDAR SPRINGS, MI

A friend fixed me up on a blind date with a guy named Calvin. I tried name association to remember it—Calvin Coolidge. But when I said good night, the only president I could think of was Grover Cleveland.

E. ANNE CAPRON · SHEFFIELD, TX

Bob Hope hams it up with Jerry Colonna.

HOPE YOU DON'T LIKE VARIETY

Bob Hope was entertaining troops in the South Pacific while I was with the 1st Marine Division on Pavuvu in the Solomon Islands in 1944. He wanted to get home after performing at Guadalcanal, but he stopped at Pavuvu when he learned that we were preparing for combat. Comedian Jerry Colonna performed that day, too. I still remember one of the routines.

Bob: "What did you have for lunch?"

Jerry: "A for-goodness-sake sandwich."

Bob: "What's that?"

Jerry: "A slice of bread between two slices of bread."

Bob: "For goodness' sake!"

Jerry: "That's right."

SAMUEL WINSTEAD · LEASBURG, NC

BRAKE FLUID PUTS A STOP TO THEIR FUN

AS SOON AS I GRADUATED IN 1965, I went to work at a local gas station. The owner, Bob, had an idea that he could increase sales if he had young ladies pumping gas. He paid my friend Kathy and me $1 an hour to work every Sunday afternoon. Back then, all stations were full service, so he trained us in how to check and replenish fluids and do other duties for a service stop.

Business picked up, and we were having a good time. We particularly enjoyed it when guys would drive up, lean back in the driver's seat and smugly ask us to check the transmission fluid, only to have their smug looks turn to surprise when we'd tell them to start the car and put it in neutral.

One day the wife of a local used-car dealer drove up in her new Cadillac. Kathy checked it over and filled the transmission fluid, which was low. She was proud because she'd serviced the car of a prominent person.

Imagine our shock when we reported for work the next Sunday and we were fired! Turns out Kathy had used brake fluid instead of transmission fluid, and Bob was facing a lawsuit for damages. Oh well, it was fun while it lasted.

SANDI CIOSEK · WILMINGTON, DE

PERFECTLY POISED

For many summers in a row, we were thrilled when Dad brought out the box containing our pool's canvas liner, connecting pipes and plastic corners. Preparing to "dive" into our swanky, barely aboveground pool in Grand Island, Nebraska, in 1969, my sister Julie, 9, and I were undeterred by its 6 to 8 inches of icy water.

JON RANARD
IOWA CITY, IA

THAT HOUSEBREAKER GAVE THEM THE SLIP

ONE NIGHT BACK IN 1969, recently divorced, I was busy in the kitchen of my newly rented house while my daughters, ages 5 and 2, slept in a nearby room.

I heard a noise that sounded as if the 5-year-old had fallen out of bed. As I rounded the corner to check on her, I saw in the glow of the night light a huge snake coiled in the doorway that led to where the girls were sleeping.

Transfixed, I stood there until the snake slithered away, then I leapt into the room, grabbed both girls out of bed, took another leap to a coffee table and deposited them on a couch. They were still half asleep. (To this day I don't know how I managed to do it all so quickly.) I got on the phone to my mother to take the kids for the night. Then I called the police.

I loudly declared, "I have a snake in my bedroom!"

Chuckles on the other end. "What's his name?"

Near hysteria, I managed to convince the dispatcher that I was serious. Two officers arrived and did a thorough search of the room, pulling out drawers, lifting the mattress and poking through the closet, but after several minutes, it became something of a circus. At one point, an officer pulled a belt from the closet and, putting a finger to his lips to warn me to be quiet, slid it along the other officer's back. The poor man jumped about 3 feet in the air.

They looked for almost an hour but found nothing and left. And soon after, so did I, escaping to my parents' place.

The next morning I called my landlord, who met me at the house toting four rat traps.

"But it was a snake," I told him, "not a rat!" *Will this madness never end?*

Despite my doubts, I got home that night to find the snake caught in the traps. Using a rake, the landlord picked it up, traps still attached, and carried it outside. The thing was almost 5 feet long—my landlord thoughtfully mailed me a picture.

We never did figured out how that snake got in, though I had no more problems with reptiles. The story, however, doesn't quite end there: At my request, the landlord sent the snake's mugshot to the police station, where I hope they posted it as evidence of my bedroom terrorist.

JUDA WOODS-HAMLIN
VINCENNES, IN

A Bird in the Hand

When they tell you to ride the ostrich, you learn to wing it.

——

Racing ostriches was the half-time entertainment at the Channel City Horse Show in Santa Barbara, California, in 1963. The owner of the big birds had brought them to the Earl Warren Showgrounds with the understanding that the manager would drum up some volunteers crazy enough to ride them. I was one of the people he called.

As I waited to enter the arena, a farrier offered some sage advice. "Those guys kick out to the side, so you best stay behind them," he told me. "Last week I saw a bird kick in the wheel of a Porsche with one strike."

Up to that point the whole thing had seemed like such a lark. Suddenly I feared that great harm might befall me, but it was too late to back out. Half a dozen ostriches were waiting for their riders, so I marched into the ring with the other fools.

The stands were packed. My ostrich was struggling with two stewards who were holding it by a leather strap fastened around its middle.

"Hurry up," one steward hollered, "we can't hold it much longer. Just grab the strap and jump on from behind."

Half an hour earlier I had circled the show ring in dignified fashion, formally dressed in horse-show chic, as I put an Appaloosa through his paces in the Western pleasure horse class.

Now the crowd roared as the ostriches took center stage. They were comical just to look at. Turned loose with greenhorn riders, the birds were whipped into a racing frenzy by a cowboy on horseback, who yelled and waved a broom with zealous glee.

The gait of a two-legged creature is decidedly different from a horse's. It bobs back and forth, left to right. My mount saw a rope lying on the tanbark and jumped over it. What a very strange sensation!

We'd arranged ahead of time for a steward to pass me an ostrich egg in secret after I dismounted, which I managed with difficulty. When my bird squatted, I casually slipped the egg under it. Laughter erupted when the ostrich stood up again.

The whole ostrich gig was a success, with birds and riders receiving a standing ovation. Shortly after that show, I learned I was pregnant with my third child. For months, whenever anyone mentioned my pregnancy, my husband joked, "I don't think she's pregnant. I think she caught something from those damned ostriches."

JUDY PEARCE · CARPINTERIA, C

Sneaky Grin

My grandfather Aaron Birky was quite the prankster. In a photo of his sister Barbara, seated, with two friends taken in 1910 at their home near Hopedale, Illinois, Grandpa steals the limelight.

JULIE WHORTEN · GOODFIELD, IL